SECOND EDITION

Public Speaking 3.0

TECHNOLOGY & 21ST CENTURY PRESENTATIONS

Sherwyn P. Morreale ▶ Janice G. Thorpe

University of Colorado Colorado Springs

Kendall Hunt
publishing company

Kendall Hunt
publishing company

www.kendallhunt.com
Send all inquiries to:
4050 Westmark Drive
Dubuque, IA 52004-1840

Brief Table of Contents

Public Speaking 3.0, Second Edition Preface And Unique Features   ix

Acknowledgements   xi

PART I: UNDERSTANDING COMPETENT PUBLIC SPEAKING   1

Introducing Ethics and Competent Public Speaking   2

Preparing Your Speech Competently   4

Presenting Your Speech Competently   7

Managing Public Speaking Anxiety   9

Preparing and Presenting Your First Speech   11

Big Ideas from Part One   14

Individual and Group Activities   15

PART II: UNDERSTANDING PRESENTATIONS IN THE 21st CENTURY   19

Digital Visual Literacy   20

Images and Vision Science   23

Basic Design Principles   29

An Exercise to Practice Visualization   33

PART III: DESIGNING PRESENTATIONS USING THE "*SCRAP*" APPROACH AND OTHER TECHNIQUES   35

Simplifying Visual Design   35

Integrating Big Ideas from Parts II and III   56

Visual Aid Redesign Exercise   57

PART IV: BUILDING PRESENTATIONS IN THE 21st CENTURY   63

Building Presentations with PowerPoint   64

Exercises to Improve Your PowerPoint Slides   95

Building Presentations with Prezi   98

Exercises to Improve Your Prezi 119

Our Final Thoughts About Prezi, PowerPoint,
and *Public Speaking* 3.0 120

PART V: DELIVERING 21st CENTURY PRESENTATIONS 123

Changes in 21st Century Audiences 124

Before the Presentation 129

During the Presentation 136

After the Presentation 145

Index 151

Contents

Public Speaking 3.0, Second Edition Preface And Unique Features   ix

Acknowledgements   xi

PART I: Understanding Competent Public Speaking   1

  Introducing Ethics and Competent Public Speaking   2

    Ethics and Public Speaking   3

    The NCA Model for Public Speaking Competence   3

  Preparing Your Speech Competently   4

    Choosing and Narrowing a Speech Topic   4

    Developing a Purpose and Thesis Statement   5

    Researching and Supporting Your Speech   5

    Organizing and Outlining Your Speech   6

  Presenting Your Speech Competently   7

    Communicating with Words   7

    Communicating with Your Voice   8

    Communicating Nonverbally   8

  Managing Public Speaking Anxiety   9

    Anxiety is Learned!   10

    Unlearning Anxiety   11

  Preparing and Presenting Your First Speech   11

  Big Ideas from Part One   14

  Individual and Group Activities   15

  Glossary   18

  Endnotes   18

PART II: Understanding Presentations in the 21st Century   19

  Digital Visual Literacy   20

    What Is It?   20

    Why Is It Important?   21

    But Is It Really Worth the Effort?   22

Images and Vision Science   **23**

   Pictures Are Better   24

   Something's Missing   24

   Symbols Help   26

   Finding Good Images   27

Basic Design Principles   **29**

   Getting Started by Visualizing   30

An Exercise to Practice Visualization   **33**

Glossary   **33**

Endnotes   **34**

**PART III: Designing Presentations Using the "SCRAP" Approach
and Other Techniques**   **35**

Simplifying Visual Design   **35**

   The *SCRAP* Approach   36

      Simplicity   36

      Contrast   37

      Repetition   40

      Alignment   41

      Proximity   43

   Structuring Text Effectively   44

   Keywording   46

   Keywording Exercise   46

   Parallelism   46

   Fonts   47

   Type Size   48

   Displaying Data Effectively   49

   Tables   50

   Figures   51

   Data Visualization   55

Integrating Big Ideas from Parts II and III   **56**

Visual Aid Redesign Exercises   **57**

Glossary   **60**

Endnotes   **61**

PART IV: Building Presentations in the 21ˢᵗ Century   **63**

Building Presentations with PowerPoint   **64**

Creating Basic Slides   65

Inserting Pictures and Objects   67

Enhancing Slides   72

Building Tables and Figures   78

Adding Animation   84

Generating Your Slide Show   90

Exercises to Improve Your PowerPoint Slides   **95**

Building Presentations with Prezi   **98**

Getting Started with Prezi   98

Inserting Pictures and Objects   103

Enhancing your Prezi   106

Creating Your Presentation Path   110

Presenting Your Prezi   112

Sharing Your Prezi   115

Exercises to Improve Your Prezi   **119**

Our Final Thoughts About Prezi, PowerPoint, and *Public Speaking 3.0*   **120**

Glossary   **121**

PART V: Delivering 21ˢᵗ Century Presentations   **123**

Changes in 21ˢᵗ Century Audiences   **124**

Audiences Now Have Different Expectations   124

Audiences   125

Audiences Want to Talk Back   125

Audiences Are Not Always in the Same Room   126

Before the Presentation   **129**

Call Your Contact   129

Plan Your Attire with Technology in Mind   130

Pack the Accessories You'll Need   131

Practice with the Technology   131

Planning for Remote/Virtual Presentations   132

During the Presentation   **136**

    Getting Started   136

    Promoting Audience Involvement   137

    Managing Remote/Virtual Presentations   138

    Managing In-Person Presentations   138

After the Presentation   **145**

Glossary   **148**

Endnotes   **149**

Index   **151**

Public Speaking 3.0, Second Edition
Preface And Unique Features

In the 21st century, technology plays a central role in all aspects of our lives. Most, if not all communicators in the 21st century will, at some point, give a presentation using technology—*PowerPoint, Prezi, Keynote* or some other computer software program. Certainly, you can be a great speaker without any technological "props." But often, particularly in the business world, you will be expected to know how to use basic presentation software and tools. You may be presenting in a classroom, giving a briefing or training at work, or talking to a crowd of citizens at a community meeting. You may be asked to conduct a web conference or a webinar with viewers and listeners around the world.

The purpose of this book is to fully prepare you to give any of these presentations really well, using technology to enhance and not distract from your message. After reading and applying the techniques described in this book, nobody will ever refer to your presentations as "Death by PowerPoint"—the ultimate in boring speeches.

Our unique approach focuses on big ideas for **Understanding, Designing, Building**, and **Delivering** dynamic and engaging 21st century presentations. Many other books are available that address different areas related to presentations. Some texts focus on learning public speaking skills in general—how to give a good speech. Others focus on technology and public speaking—how to improve your slides and use computerized presentation software. We put both these concepts in one place in this new second edition—how to give a good speech, and how to incorporate 21st century presentation tools in that speech.

- **Part One: "Understanding" Competent Public Speaking**

    Describes the National Communication Association's Competent Speaker Model, including four competencies for preparing a speech and four competencies for presenting a speech—the foundations for any effective speech.

- **Part Two: "Understanding" Presentations in the 21st Century**

    Explains how very "visual" people are now, and how to use basic visual design principles to the greatest advantage in your presentations. You will acquire the knowledge and skills necessary for developing effective presentations for the visually focused 21st century audiences.

- **Part Three: "Designing" Presentations Using the *SCRAP* Approach and Other Guidelines for Success**

    Teaches you how to "*Scrap the Crap!*" Our *SCRAP* Approach, of five simple design techniques, will help make all your presentations more effective and memorable: *Simplicity, Contrast, Repetition, Alignment, and Proximity.*

- **Part Four: "Building" 21st Century Presentations**

  Provides instructions and key ideas for using today's most popular digital tools for crafting presentations, whether for the classroom or the boardroom.

- **Part Five "Delivering" 21st Century Presentations**

  Tells you what you need to know and be able to perform to maximize the actual delivery of your technology-enhanced presentations.

Why Read This Book?

Public Speaking 3.0 is a lively read! Its pages are replete with colorful examples, screen shots that illustrate the design principles, and exercises to help you apply new ways of enhancing your presentations. But perhaps the most unique feature of this second edition is that it now serves as a single source for critical concepts associated with creating and delivering effective presentations using technology. Public Speaking 3.0 takes you from the beginning of the speech creation process all the way through preparing and delivering your speech using advanced technologies. This second edition now includes the foundational steps to develop your speech, visual design techniques to enhance any form of speech aid you might use, step-by-step instructions to create necessary slides, and tips to deliver your speech in a virtual environment. This book is a one-stop shopping for competent 21st century public speakers. Once you understand basic public speaking competence and basic design principles, then no matter how presentation tools change, you have the foundation for developing any presentation.

Acknowledgements

We first express our gratitude to the communication colleagues, researchers, and instructors, who, over the years, have expressed their belief in our approach to teaching public speaking and enhancing presentations using technology.

With regard to the second edition of this book, special thanks go to Kendall Hunt's leaders and staff, who skillfully guided the development and production to completion.

We also appreciate and acknowledge the use of information on building public speaking competence, originally included in *The Competent Public Speaker Speech Evaluation Manual* (National Communication Association, 2007) and *The Competent Public Speaker textbook* (Peter Lang, 2010).

Finally, as coauthors, we acknowledge and appreciate each other's commitment to this new edition.

Understanding Competent Public Speaking

Some basic ideas about competent public speaking introduced centuries ago by the Greeks and Romans are still with us today, though contemporary communication scholars and teachers may phrase those ideas a bit differently. Today we often say that competent communication means communicating in a way that is both *effective* and *appropriate* for the particular situation. Effective communication means you achieve your communicative goal or purpose, and appropriate communication means you are aware and respectful of the norms and expectations for communicating in the particular situation.

Applying this definition to public speaking, **competent public speaking** is both effective and appropriate for the particular rhetorical situation.[1] This simply means you accomplish the goal of your speech in a way that is respectful of the situation you are speaking in and the other people involved. Your choice of topic, the material you include, and your way of delivering the speech are all informed by what is going on in the particular situation. Then technically, you are a public speaker who is "rhetorically sensitive" to the audience and situation. And in the 21st century, the audience and situation have definitely changed, which bring us to the title of this book.

We titled this text *Public Speaking 3.0* for a specific reason. *Public Speaking 1.0* originated with Aristotle and the great orators who founded the discipline of communication—they spoke without any technology—using what we could call the rhetorical tradition. Two thousand years later, around 1950 or so, *Public Speaking 2.0* emerged. This transformation involved using electricity and special equipment to project information or pictures to a screen. For those of you born after 1990, here is an example of *Public Speaking 2.0* equipment known as an overhead projector. You may never have seen or used a projector that looks like this one.

A short 30 years or so later, we arrived at *Public Speaking 3.0*. The evolution to 3.0 has largely been the result of a combination of forces related to the Internet and the ease and availability of images and image manipulation software. But we're getting ahead of ourselves. Before you even begin to think about the software you might use to start developing your slides, you first need to understand some simple but critical concepts associated with competent public speaking.

▼ **Competent Public Speaking**
is both effective and appropriate for the particular rhetorical situation.

Figure 1.1 Forms of Pulic Speaking

▼ **Public Speaking**
involves one person or a small group of people speaking to a larger number of people, usually referred to as an audience.

Public speaking involves one person or a small group of people speaking to a larger number of people, usually referred to as an audience. Speeches have an array of different purposes and are delivered in many different ways.

The purpose of an informative speech is to communicate something new or a new perspective to an audience, and move listeners to greater understanding or insight. The purpose of a persuasive speech is to influence the audience's attitudes, beliefs, values, or behaviors. The main types of delivery can be categorized based on how much time you have to prepare, from very little time—like an impromptu speech—to a lot more time—such as an extemporaneous delivery using brief notes, or a manuscript that is read to the audience, or a memorized speech. A fifth type of delivery is a technology-aided speech and that is what this book is all about. Speeches using computerized presentation technology are probably the most popular nowadays, and they probably are the most misunderstood and misused.

To get you started right, this first part of our book introduces you to the fundamentals of public speaking by addressing these topics:

■ Introducing Ethics and Competent Public Speaking

■ Preparing Your Speech Competently

■ Presenting Your Speech Competently

■ Managing Public Speaking Anxiety

■ Preparing and Presenting Your First Speech

INTRODUCING ETHICS AND COMPETENT PUBLIC SPEAKING

One of the most important fundamentals of competent public speaking to begin with is a discussion of ethical issues. No matter how effectively you prepare and present a speech, if the listeners suspect you are not a moral and principled speaker, they won't believe or buy into anything you have to say. In fact, to be considered competent, it is critical that you communicate ethically with your audience.

Ethics and Public Speaking

Ethical communication means sharing sufficient and appropriate information with others, so they can make good decisions about matters of importance to themselves. Let's apply that general definition to public speaking. Your ethical responsibility as a public speaker is to engage in research that fully explores your topic, as you develop your speech. Then you have an ethical responsibility to fully disclose what you learn and what you know about the topic in your speech, in a forthcoming and open manner and without personal bias. The benefit to this ethical approach is that it will enhance your ethos or credibility with the audience and thus you will be perceived as a more competent speaker.

▼ **Ethical Communication** means sharing sufficient and appropriate information with others, so they can make good decisions about matters of importance to themselves.

As you now read about the steps involved in preparing and presenting your speeches, think about the possible ethical dilemmas that may confront you. If you are preparing a persuasive speech, and you discover a visual depiction of the topic that distorts what is true but is highly persuasive, what will you do? As you present the speech, would there be a way to use that visual depiction competently to get the audience involved, but at the same time, let them know there are two perspectives on the topic? That would be competent public speaking.

The NCA Model for Public Speaking Competence

The Competent Speaker is a model for public speaking developed in 1990 and revised in 2007 by the leading academic association in the Communication discipline. The National Communication Association (NCA).[2] The model consists of eight public speaking competencies, four of which relate to preparation and four to delivery. The model's eight competencies for public speaking are outlined in Table 1.1. These public speaking competencies, developed by public speaking experts, may be applied to any type of speech, from informative to persuasive and from impromptu to fully scripted. Most important, they also apply directly to how you use presentation aids and computerized presentation tools.

This first part of our book describes NCA's eight public speaking competencies individually and in detail.

TABLE 1.1 Eight Public Speaking Competencies of the National Communication Association's Competent Speaker Model

Competency One	Chooses and narrows a topic appropriately for the audience and occasion
Competency Two	Communicates the thesis/specific purpose in a manner appropriate for the audience and occasion
Competency Three	Provides supporting material (including electronic and non-electronic presentational aids) appropriate for the audience and occasion
Competency Four	Uses an organizational pattern appropriate to the topic, audience, occasion, and purpose
Competency Five	Uses language appropriate to the audience and occasion
Competency Six	Uses vocal variety in rate, pitch, and intensity (volume) to heighten and maintain interest appropriate to the audience and occasion
Competency Seven	Uses pronunciation, grammar, and articulation effectively and appropriate to the audience and occasion
Competency Eight	Uses physical behaviors that support the verbal message

Take another look at each of the competencies listed in Table 1.1, and think about which of them you already do well and which you may need to focus on and improve. We will now consider how you can apply these competencies to preparing and presenting your next speech. We also will give you some suggestions about how these competencies relate to technology and public speaking.

PREPARING YOUR SPEECH COMPETENTLY
Choosing and Narrowing a Speech Topic

▼ **Competency One** calls for choosing and narrowing a topic for your speech based on thoughtful analysis of the audience members, their needs, and interests.

You begin with **Competency One** by choosing and narrowing a topic for your speech based on thoughtful analysis of the audience members, their needs, and interests. What do your listeners know about your topic? How can you make it most relevant to them? This information will guide and shape every aspect of what you include in your speech.

Once you have analyzed your audience, then you think about things like the situation or occasion for the speech, the length requirements, and your personal knowledge of the topic you are considering. Specifically you should be able to answer such questions as:

1. Will the speaking situation influence what you say and how you say it?

2. Can you cover the topic in the time allotted?

3. Are you knowledgeable about the topic?

4. Is technology required and do you know how to use it competently? *PowerPoint, Prezi,* or something else?

1. Narrow your topic

Dusit/Shutterstock.com

Figure 1.2 Competency One

All of these questions must be considered, even when a topic is assigned by your instructor. Any topic needs to be narrowed and focused, so it appeals to the particular audience and works within the time constraints. Although this sounds simplistic, it is often a difficult step for beginning speakers. You may either try to cover a topic that is too broad and involves too much information (because five minutes sounds like an eternity!), or you may not have enough information to fill the allotted time. Learning how much you can cover in a given speech is an important part of becoming a competent public speaker.

Try this for yourself: Your first speech assignment is a self-introduction to be given in the first week of your beginning public speaking class. You have four to five minutes and are required to use some sort of visual aid. How would you answer these four questions, based on the guidelines for this assignment? Take a minute and think about your answers.

1. *Will the speaking situation influence what you say and how you say it?* Yes, it's only the first week of class, so you should not reveal too much personal information, but you do want your classmates (and your instructor) to learn something about you that they will find interesting.

2. *Can you cover the topic in the time allotted?* Yes, you could acquaint the class with who you are or what you care about by discussing your work, a hobby or favorite activity, a significant personal experience, or your professional or

academic goals. If you have only five minutes, developing only one of these as a specific topic is better than trying to cover all of them.

3. *Are you knowledgeable about the topic?* Yes, you're certainly more knowledgeable about the topic—yourself—and therefore it shouldn't require much research.

4. *Is technology required and do you know how to use it competently?* PowerPoint, *Prezi*, or something else? The assignment may call for a "visual aid" that may or may not include technology. As you're thinking about your content, also consider what you could "show" the audience to give them a better "picture" of you. If you've chosen to focus on a favorite hobby or activity—rock-climbing for example—consider bringing in a few of the pieces of equipment you use. This visual aid will be very helpful to anyone in your audience who may have absolutely no experience with this activity. Visual aids will be addressed in more detail in Competency Three.

Developing a Purpose and Thesis Statement

After choosing a specific topic, **Competency Two** says you should determine a thesis/specific purpose for your speech that you will communicate to the audience when you present. The general purpose of a speech is based on the type of speech that is assigned—a speech to inform, to persuade, or perhaps to motivate or entertain.

▼ **Competency Two** says you should determine a thesis/specific purpose for your speech that you will communicate to the audience when you present.

The specific purpose is narrower than the general purpose, and it tells the audience exactly what you will try to accomplish and where the speech is headed. The thesis statement also is stated aloud to the audience and it tells them why your topic will be of interest to them.

For example, in a self-introduction speech, your specific purpose might be, "to tell the audience about the health and recreational benefits you have experienced as a result of rock-climbing." The thesis statement you would say aloud in the introduction to the speech could be something like this:

> "By learning more about the benefits of rock climbing, you may be motivated to try a new physical fitness program for yourself."

Getting clear about your purpose and thesis may seem like a trivial competency, but it is not. Many speeches are not as effective as they could be, because the audience isn't clear about what the speech is all about and why they should care about it. If you can't clearly articulate your thesis statement, chances are the audience will not be able to identify it either.

2. Define your purpose and thesis

Bleakstar/Shutterstock.com

Figure 1.3 Competency Two

Researching and Supporting Your Speech

Competency Three encourages you to gather and provide supporting material that will help to accomplish the specific purpose of your speech. These materials should include a variety of types of information. In order to enhance your credibility, they should come from your own personal experiences but also from

▼ **Competency Three** encourages you to gather and provide supporting material that will help to accomplish the specific purpose of your speech.

3. Gather supporting material

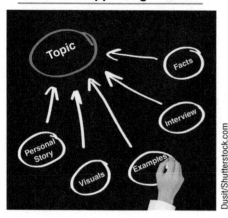

Figure 1.4 Competency Three

other outside sources. Through research in the library, electronic databases, and interviews with experts, you can find material such as statistics, facts and figures, and stories or examples that will help to make your speech appealing and memorable.

Be sure to balance the amount of hard information and data (list after list of bullet points),with the amount of personal stories and examples. Too much hard information in one speech is overwhelming to listeners and not nearly as interesting. For a speech about the benefits of rock climbing, you could get hard information from the National Institutes of Health. You also could interview the director of the rock climbing program at your gym. A personal story about one of your favorite climbs could help to introduce you in a friendly manner to the other students.

As you are researching and collecting material to include in your speech, you should also be thinking about how you will "show" your audience what you are talking about. How might you help the audience "see" how much fun you can have rock-climbing? If you do include material from an interview with a director of rock climbing, is there an image to help the audience "see" who you talked to, or what the gym and rock-climbing wall look like? As you develop the content of your speech, insert "visualization" into the speech creation process. *Visualization* is the representation of words or text with pictures, images, or symbols. Below we illustrate how visualization fits into the overall development of a speech. Notice in the circle that the arrow between *Content* and *Visualization* goes in both directions. The more you think about what image will best portray your idea, the more you have to clarify your content, so you can choose the correct images.

▼ **Visualization**
is the representation of words or text with pictures, images, or symbols.

Figure 1.5 Visualization and the Speech Development Process

Try this for yourself: As you think about what you will cover in your speech, imagine the pictures or images you might use in place of words. Think through the entire content of the speech, by visualizing what the audience will see, in addition to the words you will say.

We cover visualization in much more detail in the next chapter, with lots of examples for practicing how to visualize speech content. But for now, a final hint, keep good records as you gather support materials. Consider putting each piece of information on a separate note card. That extra effort will help you with the next preparation step, which is organizing your speech.

Organizing and Outlining Your Speech

▼ **Competency Four**
focuses on arranging your information—the support materials—in an organizational pattern that is appropriate to the topic, audience, occasion, and purpose of your speech.

Competency Four focuses on arranging your information—the support materials—in an organizational pattern that is appropriate to the topic, audience, occasion, and purpose of your speech. First, return to the specific purpose of the speech, examine the support materials and research notes you gathered, and identify two or three main points for your speech. Keep the time limit in mind as you decide on main points, and err on the side of fewer main points rather than more. Arrange the main points in a logical order and break down each main point into several subpoints. Then choose the best supporting materials for each main point and set of subpoints. Try to be creative in the use of the materials and include at least one meaningful example or impressive statistic for each main point. Now you are ready to give your speech some shape.

Many centuries ago, the great Roman orator, Cicero, advised us to divide a speech into three main sections: the introduction, body, and conclusion.

The introduction is the first section of the speech in which you capture the listeners' attention and engage them in the topic of your speech. You could use a startling quotation or a moving story as an opening device, followed by a clear statement of your specific purpose and thesis, and a preview of the content of the speech. The body of the speech consists of your main points, and clear and logical transitions among the main points. The conclusion ends the speech on a resounding and summative note. It lets the audience know the speech is over, summarizes and reinforces what you have said, and if appropriate, it motivates the audience to some kind of action. The conclusion should leave some kind of lasting impression and bring your speech to a memorable ending. Often it is helpful and effective to link the conclusion back to the attention-getting device or thesis that you stated in the introduction. That extra effort will give your entire speech a sense of connectedness from beginning to end.

To help you develop effective speech outlines, a standard outline format displaying all the essential components of an effective speech is presented at the end of this first part of our book. You can use this standard format to develop your own speech, particularly if your general purpose is to inform. A format for persuasive speeches also is presented at the end of Part One. This format, the Motivated Sequence, is used by many speakers when the purpose is to persuade or motivate the audience to change their attitudes, beliefs, values, or behaviors. Speeches with the purpose of persuading the audience can be organized using this outline format, which includes five main points or sequential steps: attention, need, satisfaction, visualization, and action.

4. Organize and outline your content

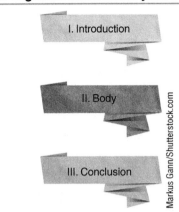

Figure 1.6 Competency Four

PRESENTING YOUR SPEECH COMPETENTLY

Once you have prepared your speech and have an outline or note cards ready, then you can begin to think about the four presentation competencies. But remember, practice the speech ahead of time, and with a live audience if at all possible.

Communicating with Words

Competency Five says you should use appropriate language for the audience and occasion. When you are up in front of an audience and have very little time, your choice of words is critical to the effectiveness of your speech. You should use language that is exceptionally *clear* to ensure audience understanding, *vivid* to ensure their enthusiasm for your speech, and *appropriate* for the particular occasion. Choose words that clarify your meaning, develop understanding, and paint mental images for your listeners. For instance, if you want to describe the intensity of your fitness training program, don't say you had to lay down for a while right after the first class. Rather, tell the audience how you "collapsed at the end of the first hour, unable to move even your little finger." Be excited about the topic and use exciting language, but choose words that are natural to you and not pretentious or condescending. Be respectful to all of your listeners and avoid words that might offend or embarrass anyone in the audience.

To ensure your words and language are most effective when you present, write out the introduction, transitions among main points,

▼ **Competency Five** says you should use appropriate language for the audience and occasion.

5. Use appropriate language

Figure 1.7 Competency Five

and the conclusion ahead of time. Put those sentences on the outline or note cards you will use to present, and memorize them. You will not read them to the audience verbatim, but you will then be able to say them in a way that is really effective.

Communicating with Your Voice

▼ **Competency Six**
says you should enliven your delivery of the speech by varying *how* you say what you say.

6. Heighten vocal variety

Volume
Rate
Pitch

R. Gino Santa Maria/Shutterstock.com

Figure 1.8 Competency Six

▼ **Competency Seven**
also focuses on how you speak but with an emphasis on effective and appropriate articulation, pronunciation, and grammar.

According to **Competency Six**, you should enliven your delivery of the speech by varying *how* you say what you say. Vary the rate or pace at which you talk, sometimes faster and sometimes slower. Vary your pitch, the highness or lowness of your voice, and vary your intensity or volume.

Use a conversational style of speaking, but at the same time, be sure you talk loud enough to be easily heard by all audience members. Speech teachers often refer to using a public voice rather than a private voice, to make sure that everyone hears you and pays attention. If you have ever sat through a lecture with an instructor using only a monotone voice, that should tell you how *not* to speak. Instead, use your voice as a tool to heighten and maintain interest in your speech and its content.

Competency Seven also focuses on how you speak but with an emphasis on effective and appropriate articulation, pronunciation, and grammar. If you mispronounce a word or you don't articulate speech sounds correctly, your listeners may not understand what you say. If your speech is full of grammatical errors, listeners will pay attention to those mistakes and not to the good content of your speech. Any such errors will have a negative effect on your credibility as a speaker, no matter how well you planned and developed the content of the speech. If you have ever been unable to understand a message left on your cell phone that would have probably resulted from the speaker not paying attention to this competency.

Communicating Nonverbally

7. Practice speaking correctly

Articulation
Pronunciation
Grammar

Figure 1.9 Competency Seven

▼ **Competency Eight**
is about understanding and using physical behaviors and nonverbal cues to support and enhance your verbal/spoken message.

Competency Eight is about understanding and using physical behaviors and nonverbal cues to support and enhance your verbal/spoken message. Like your use of language, your use of nonverbal communication has a significant impact on the audience's reaction to you and to your speech. The nonverbal cues that most impact how you are perceived as a public speaker are your posture, gestures, physical appearance, body movement, eye contact, and facial expressions.

You should modify your appearance—clothing, jewelry, and hair style—to make a favorable first impression on the audience. By making an effort to appear professional and competent, you also tell the listeners that you respect and appreciate their attention. In addition to dressing professionally, you should sit, stand, and walk with confidence, your head up and shoulders erect. Whether standing or moving, keep your hands and arms free and relaxed, so you can use gestures to reinforce and emphasize what you are saying. The important thing is to gesture naturally, not in a stilted or stylized way. Your facial expressions can be used to communicate to the listener how you feel about the topic of your speech. Be sure that your expression matches what you are saying. If the topic is a sad or serious one, it's best not to smite or grin as you are speaking. You also can use eye contact to promote a sense of audience contact and let the audience know that you are involved with them. If you avoid eye contact with your listeners, they will think you are either nervous or not interested in their reactions to your speech.

As you begin to contemplate the challenge of your next speech, here is one final suggestion that will help you immeasurably . . . speech teachers call this the "three Ps."

Prepare, prepare, prepare and then practice, practice, practice!

According to one recent study, overall preparation time resulted in significantly higher speech grades, and students who spent more time practicing their speeches also earned higher grades.[3] In another study, students who practiced their speeches before a live audience—not the family cat— got higher grades than students who practiced without an audience; and students who practiced their speech before larger audiences received higher scores than students who practiced before smaller audiences.[4] Your practicing needs to include any presentation software you intend to use. For example, make sure you know how to load and access your presentation slides onto the computer you will actually use to deliver your speech.

In addition to the eight competencies for preparing and presenting speeches, Part Five of this book specifically discusses the delivery skills needed for the 21st century presentations using technology, including in a virtual environment. However, before moving our discussion to technology and public speaking, one more challenge most speakers face that needs to be addressed is the public speaking jitters!

8. Monitor physical behaviors

Posture

Gestures

Appearance

Movement

Eye contact

Facial expression

Figure 1.10 Competency Eight

MANAGING PUBLIC SPEAKING ANXIETY

Most people become a little bit nervous at the very thought of giving a speech. Communication instructors find these reactions to be relatively normal and refer to this challenge as public speaking anxiety. Public speaking anxiety refers to a

▼ **Public speaking anxiety** refers to a person's level of fear or anxiety associated with a real or anticipated public speaking event.

"I turn pale at the outset of a speech, and quake in every limb and in all my soul."

Figure 1.11 Cicero, The Great Roman Orator

person's level of fear or anxiety associated with a real or anticipated public speaking event. If you have not learned to manage your speech anxiety, then all the preparation in the world will not ensure that you present your speech effectively. What's worse, if this anxiety causes you to delay and put off preparing your speech, some researchers tell us that your anxiety will actually be much worse.[5] To address this challenge to public speaking competence, let's now talk about what public speaking anxiety is, how we all learned to be anxious, and how we can unlearn it.

Anyone who has experienced nervous anticipation prior to presenting a speech understands public speaking anxiety without any further explanation. The great Roman orator we mentioned earlier, Cicero, suffered from terrible public speaking anxiety. He confessed, *"I turn pale at the outset of a speech, and quake in every limb and in all my soul."*

Because he did become a great orator, Cicero proved that if you harness and overcome your inner feelings of nervousness, you'll become a better speaker for it. Furthermore, Cicero also is evidence that having some anxiety, at least a little, may be positive. A manageable amount of anxiety indicates that you understand and take seriously your responsibilities as a public speaker. Indeed, speech instructors tell us that overly confident students often underperform, by comparison to students whose levels of anxiety encourage them to work hard to develop their public speaking skills.

Let's first think about why we are anxious about public speaking in the first place. By knowing why anxiety occurs and how you learned to have it, you can be better prepared to use some anxiety-reducing techniques for unlearning it.

Anxiety is Learned!

One cause of anxiety is remembering negative experiences that happened to you in the past when you spoke in public.

Figure 1.12 First Reason

Figure 1.14 Third Reason

It may have been something trivial, like answering a question incorrectly in an elementary school class and others laughed or made fun of you. Or it may have been more significant, like presenting a speech and having the audience strongly disagree and challenge your remarks in public. In any case, the lesson was learned: "When I speak in public, I feel foolish or stupid."

A second cause of anxiety is identifying with ineffective public speakers as your role models, rather than effective speakers. You watch someone speak on television or at a meeting who makes mistakes or who is poorly organized. You identify with that person or perhaps with another nervous student, rather than with someone who speaks effectively and impressively. You say to yourself, now that's the kind of speaker I am. The lesson is learned: "When I speak in public, I am uncomfortable and make embarrassing mistakes."

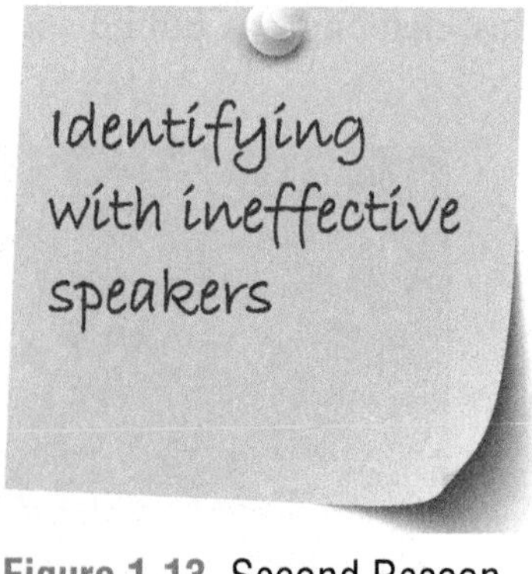

A third cause of public speaking anxiety is holding negative and unrealistic expectations about public speaking in general and about yourself as a public speaker. For example, you may have the expectation that your speech is going to be a big disaster, a catastrophic failure. You expect something awful to happen, like forgetting everything you plan to say. Or, you may have an unrealistic desire to be totally accepted and liked by all

Figure 1.13 Second Reason

Figure 1.15 Conquer Your Fear

the listeners in the audience. Your speech needs to be perceived by the audience as perfect and flawless in every way, no mistakes.

You also may expect that you should feel completely confident, calm, and in control. All of these expectations are unrealistic and again, a negative lesson is learned: "I cannot possibly be a good public speaker and the audience won't like me or the speech."

Yes, you can conquer any fear of public speaking you may have by concentrating on the listeners and your important message for them, and not on yourself!

Unlearning Anxiety

Now that you know some of the causes of public speaking anxiety, you can consider how to unlearn and manage it. The key is to control the anxiety, so it doesn't take over and distract you from doing a good job of your speech. You need to learn how to use the nervousness about giving a speech as a way to energize your presentation.

Table 1.2 summarizes the causes of public speaking anxiety we just described, how people react to each cause, and some solutions for each of the negative reactions. See which cause you relate to the most and make note of the suggestions for handling that cause and its reaction.

PREPARING AND PRESENTING YOUR FIRST SPEECH

You now know what it means to be a really awesome public speaker—what some communication instructors refer to as a highly competent communicator. If you apply the eight public speaking competencies to your next speech, you may be surprised to notice that you do so with more confidence and less anxiety. No matter what the next speech assignment is, prepare for it carefully. Choose the right topic, focus your purpose and thesis statement, engage in thorough research for support materials, and develop a solid presentation outline. Then practice the speech ahead of time, preferably before a live audience even if that is only one

TABLE 1.2 Public Speaking Anxiety: Causes, Reactions, and Solutions

Cause	Reaction	Possible Solution
Previous negative experiences with public speaking	Avoid public speaking so you won't look foolish and stupid	Forget the past and don't allow it to shape the present
Identification with the wrong role models	Avoid public speaking because you'll make mistakes and embarrass yourself	Make a conscious effort to identify with speakers who appear confident and in control. Watch those people and think about yourself being a public speaker just like them
Unrealistic expectations about public speaking and premonition of disaster or catastrophic failure	Avoid public speaking because you can't possibly do well	Realize that it is unlikely that anything catastrophic will occur. And if something does go wrong, it isn't the end of the world
	Desire for total acceptance	Realize it's impossible to please everyone all the time, just as it's impossible for everyone to please you all the time. Be yourself and do the best job you can
	Desire for absolute perfection	Don't expect perfection. Realize that no speech is perfect, then accept your imperfections and learn from mistakes. Don't dwell on what goes wrong
	Desire for total confidence	Expect anxiety. Realize that fear is natural and everyone has it. Accept your insecurities, knowing the audience can't see your fears and they are probably supportive of you

person. Pay attention to any feedback about how you use words and language, your voice, and all sorts of nonverbal cues. If you don't have access to a willing listener, consider taping or recording your speech, and become your own best critic.

Regarding speech critics, the information in Table 1.3 tells you what *not* to do when you present your next speech. Speech teachers themselves compiled the list of "pet peeves"—the main things that students should avoid doing when giving speeches in their classes.

Then we end our discussion of public speaking competence by returning to where we began this first part of our book—talking about ethics and public speaking. Please consider the ethical responsibilities outlined in Table 1.4, for you as a speaker and for you as a listener in the audience. Both the speaker and the listener have ethical responsibilities that come into play at any public speaking event.

TABLE 1.3 Speech Teachers' Pet Peeves About Students' Presentations

1. **General rules of procedure on speech days** (attire, absenteeism, reading manuscripts)

   ➤ Inappropriate attire (exposed midriff, holes in jeans, hats or dirty, rumpled clothing)

   ➤ Students who are not prepared on the assigned speech day

2. Practices to avoid during the introduction and conclusion

   ➤ Beginning a speech with "Ok, ah . . ."

   ➤ Apologizing or making excuses for not being prepared at the beginning of the speech

   ➤ Beginning a speech with "Hello, my speech is on . . ."

   ➤ Beginning a speech with a really simplistic question ("How many of you . . .")

   ➤ Saying "in conclusion"

   ➤ Ending a speech with "Thank you"

   ➤ Ending a speech with "Are there any questions?"

3. **Delivery issues (vocalized pauses, slang, profanity, chewing gum)**

   ➤ Vocalized pauses (ah, um, you know, like . . .)

   ➤ Slang and profanity

   ➤ Chewing gum while speaking

   ➤ Tongue piercing clicking against teeth

   ➤ Citing as a legitimate source: Yahoo, Google, the Internet, the Web, or Wikipedia

4. **Ineffective use of presentation aids**

   ➤ Poorly prepared visuals

   ➤ Passing photos or other visuals around during the speech

   ➤ Using the podium as a conga drum

   ➤ Standing in front of the projection screen or other visuals

   ➤ Talking to the visual aid rather than the audience

   ➤ Visual aids that are alive

5. **Miscellaneous peeves**

   ➤ Language that sounds sexist, biased or uses stereotypes

   ➤ Speeches written out on notebook paper

   ➤ Controversial speech topics like abortion, gun control, or marijuana (unless instructor approved)

Source: Speech Teachers' Pet Peeves (Taylor, K. 2005, Florida Communication Journal).

Table 1.4 Public Speaking Ethical Responsibilities: For Speakers and Listeners

Speaker's Responsibilities

1. Always come prepared to address your audience. Don't offend your listeners by trying to "wing it" during a presentation. They will know if you are not prepared

2. Be considerate of time. Your listeners have taken time out of their day to be your audience. The planners have allotted you a specific window of time, do not go overtime

3. Dress professionally. Show respect for your listeners by dressing appropriately. Men should wear a collared shirt and slacks. Women should wear a dress, or slacks or a skirt, with a professional blouse. No jeans, no tee-shirts, no tennis shoes or flip flops for either sex. You may distract the listeners from your message with too casual an appearance

4. Look at your audience and speak with a strong, public voice. It's your job to ensure all listeners can see and hear you throughout your speech.

5. Finally, be prepared for anything that may go wrong; technology isn't perfect. The flash drive might fail or the computer could shut down. Plan for the unexpected

Listener's Responsibilities

1. Be respectful and arrive on time. Find a seat and be in it before the speaker begins talking

2. Turn off your cell phone, pager, beeper, or blackberry. If absolutely necessary, turn the device to vibrate so calls won't interrupt the presentation

3. Do not get up and leave or enter the room during a presentation

4. Wait until there is a pause in the presentation before opening up your briefcase or backpack or purse. These activities make noise and can distract from the speech

5. Do not eat or drink or send or receive text messages, while the speaker is presenting

6. Show respect for the speakers by listening and looking at them directly during their presentation

7. Focus your full attention on the speaker's message and prepare to participate in a Q&A after the speech. If you expect others to listen to you, then be prepared to do the same

Source: Marcelle Hureau and Corlea Keeney, University of Colorado at Colorado Springs (2009).

BIG IDEAS FROM PART ONE

The most important ideas to remember and be able to do from Part One are these eight public speaking competencies, developed by the National Communication Association:

Competency One calls for choosing and narrowing a topic for your speech based on thoughtful analysis of the audience and their needs and interests.

Competency Two says you should determine a thesis/specific purpose for your speech that you will communicate to the audience when you present.

Competency Three encourages you to gather and provide supporting material that will help to accomplish the specific purpose of your speech.

Competency Four focuses on arranging your information—the support materials—in an organizational pattern that is appropriate to the topic, audience, occasion, and purpose of your speech.

Competency Five says you should use appropriate language for the audience and occasion. When you are up in front of an audience and have very little time, your choice of words is critical to the effectiveness of your speech.

Competency Six tells you to enliven your delivery of the speech by varying how you say and what you say.

Competency Seven focuses on how you speak but with an emphasis on effective and appropriate pronunciation, grammar, and articulation.

Competency Eight is about understanding and using physical behaviors and nonverbal cues to support and enhance your verbal/spoken message.

INDIVIDUAL AND GROUP ACTIVITIES

Individual Activities

1. Attend a live lecture or speech. Analyze the speech based on the following questions and write a one-page summary of your analysis of the speech.

   ■ What was the general purpose of the speech (informative or persuasive) and what was the speaker's specific purpose and thesis?

   ■ How effective was the speaker in achieving his or her purpose?

   ■ What type of delivery was used and was it used effectively?

   ■ Was the speech delivered effectively and appropriately?

2. Go to the website of the Voices of Democracy: The U.S. Oratory Project at http://voicesofdemocracy.umd.edu/. You will find great speeches organized by speaker and by theme. Choose one speech, read it, and analyze it based on the four preparation competencies outlined in the Competent Speaker model.

3. Read over the various approaches for managing public speaking anxiety. Thank about your own personal level of the "jitters" and write a one-page summary of how you plan to approach public speaking in the future.

Group Activities

1. Form groups of four to five students. Attend a live lecture or speech. Analyze the speech based on your impression of how well the speaker used the eight public speaking competencies summarized in this chapter. Present your analysis to the class and discuss the strengths and weaknesses of the speech that you attended.

2. With a partner, access the White House website (http://www.whitehouse. gov) and find the web page that provides manuscripts of the president's recent major speeches. Select a speech that interests both of you. Prepare and present an analysis of it in class.

3. Form groups of four to five students. Share examples of significant competent or incompetent public speeches that you have attended. These could be in-class lectures. Develop a list of characteristics and behaviors of competent and incompetent public speakers based on the group discussion. Present your list of characteristics and behaviors to the class.

4. Form groups of four to five students. Share examples of significant ethical or unethical public speakers or speeches you have observed. Develop a description of the ethical speakers and unethical speakers based on the group discussion. Present your two lists to the class.

Standard Speech Outline

Speech Title: (indicate the speech topic, pique curiosity, and be concise)

General Purpose: (to inform, persuade, or entertain)

Specific Purpose: (infinitive statement indicating the goal of the speech)

INTRODUCTION (written out in full sentences)

I.   Attention-getting or lead-in device

II. Thesis statement (declarative sentence stating the central idea or claim of the speech and its significance to the audience)

III. Preview of main points

BODY (support material that accomplishes the speech purpose organized into three to four main points with subpoints for each main point)

I. First main point (can be written out as a complete sentence)

  A. First subpoint

    1. Support material

      a. Support material

      b. Support material

    2. Support material

      a. Support material

      b. Support material

  B. Second subpoint

    1. Support material

      a. Support material

      b. Support material

    2. Support material

      a. Support material

      b. Support material

***Transition** to next main point

II. Second main point (can be written out as a complete sentence)

    A. subpoint

    B. subpoint

    *Transition to next main point or to conclusion

CONCLUSION (written out in full sentences)

I.   Review of main points

II. Restatement of the thesis statement

III. Closing device

Motivated Sequence Outline

Speech Title: (indicate the issue of persuasion, pique curiosity, and be concise)

General Purpose: (to persuade)

Specific Purpose: (infinitive statement indicating the goal of the speech, to influence the audience's beliefs, attitudes, values, or behaviors about a need or problem)

Five Sequential Steps

INTRODUCTION

I.   ATTENTION STEP: Grab the audience's attention and forecast the theme of speech

BODY

II. NEED/PROBLEM: Describe the problem or need, provide evidence of its importance, and relate it to the audience's desires and/or needs

III. SATISFACTION/SOLUTION STEP: Present a plan of action to address the problem or the need

CONCLUSION

IV. VISUALIZATION STEP: Describe the results of the proposed plan or consequences of the audience's failure to change or to act

V. ACTION STEP: Summarize main ideas and call for the audience to change their beliefs or to act or react in the desired manner

GLOSSARY

Competent public speaking is both effective and appropriate for the particular rhetorical situation.

The *body of the speech* consists of your main points, and clear and logical transitions among the main points.

The *conclusion* ends the speech on a resounding and summative note.

Ethical communication means sharing sufficient and appropriate information with others, so they can make good decisions about matters important to themselves.

The *introduction* is the first section of the speech in which you capture the listeners' attention and engage them in the topic of your speech.

Public speaking involves one person or a small group of people speaking to a larger number of people, usually referred to as an audience.

Public speaking anxiety refers to a person's level of fear or anxiety associated with a real or anticipated public speaking event.

The *specific purpose* is narrower than the general purpose, and it tells the audience exactly what you will try to accomplish and where the speech is headed.

The *thesis statement* is stated aloud to the audience and it tells them why your topic will be of interest to them.

Visualization is the representation of words or text with pictures, images, or symbols.

ENDNOTES

[1] Morreale, S. P. (2010). *The Competent public speaker: A textbook*. NY: Peter Lang Publishers.

[2] Morreale, S., Moore, M., Surges-Tatum, D., & Webster, L. (2007). The competent speaker speech evaluation program, 2nd ed. Washington, DC: National Communication Association Non-Serial Publications Program.

[3] Pearson, J.C., Child, J. T., & Kahl, D. H. Jr. (2006). Preparation meeting opportunity: How do college students prepare for public speeches? *Communication Quarterly, 54*(3), 351–366.

[4] Smith, T. E. & Frymier, A. B. (2006). Get 'real': Does practicing speeches before an audience improve performance? *Communication Quarterly, 54*(1), 111–125.

[5] Behnke, R. R., & Sawyer, C. R. (1999). Public speaking procrastination as a correlate of public speaking communication apprehension and self-perceived public speaking competence. *Communication Research Reports, 16*(1), 40–47.

Understanding Presentations in the 21ˢᵗ Century

In Part I, we presented eight fundamental competencies for competent public speaking. As part of those competencies, we introduced the concept of Visualization, which is the representation of words or text with pictures, images, or symbols. In public speaking, visualization is more than just choosing an interesting picture for your slides. Fundamentally, it's about helping your listeners to more clearly "see" the content of your speech instead of just "hearing" it. 21st century public speakers need to be aware of this increasing visual orientation, as it relates to their audiences and adapt their speech preparation and practice to match the 21st century audience.

Since the advent of television, each successive generation has become more visually focused, more influenced by what they see than what they hear or feel. Public speakers in the 21ˢᵗ century need to be aware of this increasing visual orientation, as it relates to their audiences. The latest named generation, *Millennials* and *Generation C*—those born in 1990 or later—are accustomed to information packaged with high resolution and high speed graphics.

This increasing *visualness* has generated an emerging field of study, known as *Digital Visual Literacy*. Much like reading literacy, and writing literacy, Digital Visual Literacy is quickly becoming an essential skill in many areas of our daily lives. Activities such as reading a newspaper, surfing the web, writing a business report, or creating a presentation all call for some understanding of visuality and imagery.

An excerpt from an article by Spalter and van Dam summarizes this evolution:

> To give an idea of the degree to which the digital visual world has evolved, note that Kodak no longer makes film cameras or slide carousels, and Adobe Photoshop™ is now commonly used as a verb. We have traded in our bulky black dial phones from about 20 years ago for sleek cell phones that now work all over the globe. Some contain megapixel cameras whose pictures we can beam to family, friends, websites, or even, in New York City, to 911.[1]

Figure 2.1 Millennials and Images

DIGITAL VISUAL LITERACY

What Is It?

▼ **Digital Visual Literacy** suggests two critical abilities or components: 1) the ability to analyze and interpret data and 2) the ability to create images to communicate messages.

Consensus on a definition of ***digital visual literacy*** does not exist, but a review of many definitions suggests two critical abilities or components: 1) the ability to analyze and interpret data and 2) the ability to create images to communicate messages. These two core components are clarified in the list below. The 21st century speaker should:

- Understand basic visual design elements

- Recognize emotional, psychological, physiological, and cognitive influences in perceptions of visuals

- Comprehend explanatory, abstract, and symbolic images

- Be informed consumers of visual information

- Be able to effectively communicate using visual imagery

21st Century Skills: Literacy in the Digital Age[2]

Including a chapter on visual literacy in this book is essential for two reasons. Recognizing the role of visual literacy will help bring a discussion of visual aids to a more conscious and deliberate level. Too often, visual aids are an afterthought. Once the outline and notes for a speech are completed, then speakers convert that information to a poster, slides, or a handout, and the results may be less than exceptional. Certainly the content and organization of your ideas are critical for an effective presentation, but these tasks are NOT separate from the visual components necessary to effectively present your ideas. As you learned in Part I, Visualization is a vital part of your development process, as you research and gather your supporting materials (Competency Three). Once you learn more about digital visual literacy and how it functions in the speech development process, you will more likely consider design issues earlier and as integral to your content.

The second reason to begin with a discussion of digital visual literacy is to provide you with the skills necessary to create visually appealing presentation aids. Just being aware of design issues when creating a speech will not ensure you create visually appealing slides or handouts. It is important to learn and practice the basic skills to take your slides from boring and dull, to "Wow! That was awesome." Do not worry if you're not a trained artist—most speakers aren't. But you can learn basic visual literacy principles and, when combined with practice, those principles will help you design and create better visual aids.

Much research shows that even if you have been creating presentations since middle school, you may not have been taught visual literacy skills, which are different from technology skills. Learning to use a certain software package, even those intended for presentations or graphic design, is not the same as instruction on visual design. A recent study of Millennial learners found 75 percent of the participants considered themselves somewhat or very skilled with presentation software such as Microsoft® PowerPoint®, and a handful of them (8 percent) described themselves as having

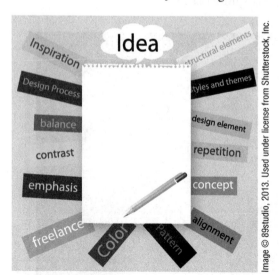

Image © 89studio, 2013. Used under license from Shutterstock, Inc.

Figure 2.2 Design Concepts

expert/professional level skills.[3] These results are similar to other studies that also show students feel they are fairly competent in using various computer presentation tools.[4] However, these studies also found that just because students reported some experience with presentation software, that didn't necessarily correspond with high skill levels. Only 8 percent of respondents said that they frequently download slide designs or templates from the web, and only 13 percent said they frequently design their own slides or templates. In other words, the vast majority are simply using the pre-existing templates that come with their software rather than searching for or developing more innovative, creative, or appropriate designs.

Obviously, there is a disconnect between the ability to use a certain presentation tool at a basic level and knowing the design elements needed to produce visually appealing and creative images. Software packages and technology alone will not produce a visually appealing, professional presentation. Rather, a good starting point is the underlying design principles needed to enhance the reception and retention of your message.

Yet in most public speaking courses, there just is not enough time to adequately cover the visual principles and theories critical to good presentations. Most courses can only devote one or maybe two lecture periods to visual aids. There is little to no time left for considering the design theory that is increasingly important for communicating in the 21st century.

Why Is It Important?

Visual Literacy has been suggested by economists, employers, and educators, as a key skill for the 21st century.[5] Countless articles suggest there has been a cultural shift from an emphasis on print media to digital media. Many causes account for this shift, but two are most significant: The increase in tools that allow for more direct control over creating and altering our own content and images; and, of course, the rise of the Internet. Anyone can now take a picture and edit the photo using various software products. And we do this editing right in our own homes with equipment that costs just a few hundred dollars. With an Internet connection, anyone, anywhere in the world, can view our work. It's now fairly inexpensive and very easy to create and share visual images. But that does not mean we have become better creators of these visual images, just because it is cheaper and easier to produce them.

Spalter and Dam share this concern:

> The design bar has been raised and design skills are more and more prerequisite for today's students. The availability of powerful design tools to anyone with a personal computer cuts both ways: people can easily create materials at home that would once have required a graphic design firm, but now that so many people touchup their own photographs, design their own cards, and print correspondence on crisp high resolution printers, work begins to look somehow amateurish and deficient when these tools are not used.[6]

OK, unless you're majoring in art or graphic design, it's unlikely you've been taught the design principles we will be talking about. But the need to understand design is no longer limited to art classes. Students from all disciplines, Engineering, Business Sciences, Humanities, and especially those studying Communication, must recognize the impact

Figure 2.3 Software Tools

of visual images in our society. No matter what your intended career, it's likely you'll need to have some grasp of digital visual literacy and some ability to use that knowledge to create effective presentations. And since more and more non-designers have access to the tools and equipment to create print and digital media, learning about visual design principles is more important than ever. Figure 2.4 shows two slides—the slide on the left is very text-heavy and extremely dull. The slide on the right uses images to represent the three forces instead of words. It is up to the speaker to provide evidence and examples to explain the three forces to the audience. Using the images, combined with animation to build the screen as the speaker narrates, would be far better for the audience than the text only slide. As a matter of fact, the slide on the left results in the speaker becoming virtually irrelevant. The side-by-side comparison of these two slides clearly illustrates the importance of visual design—one is grounded in sound principles of visual design and the other slide is the "before shot!"

But Is It Really Worth the Effort?

Learning a new skill or new software program definitely requires an investment of your time and effort. The central question is: "Is it worth it for you? If I'm a really good speaker, and I keep the audience interested and focused on me, why do I need visual aids at all?" Here are several reasons to pay just as much attention to your visual aids as you do to your speech outline:

1. The primary reason you need to use visual aids is to be more effective.

Many studies suggest presentations using visual aids are more effective. Two in particular clearly demonstrate the positive effects of using visuality in presentations. One study, at the 3M/Wharton School at University of Pennsylvania, highlighted the positive effects of using overhead transparencies in business meetings.[7] Another study, conducted at the University of Minnesota/3M, underscored the critical role of visual presentation in supporting effective persuasion.[8]

2. Visual aids add another sensory channel to the oral communication process.

Other researchers say that people tend to learn in three ways, that there are three different learning styles: verbal (what you hear—the words), visual (what you see), and kinesthetic (what you feel).[9] In the past, presentations were mostly verbal and only recently have audiences expected a visual component as well.

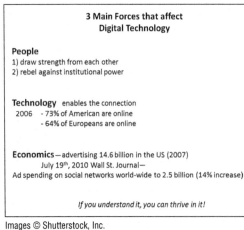

Images © Shutterstock, Inc.

Figure 2.4 Before and After Slides

Adding a visual component adds a second sensory channel for communicating your message to the listeners, some of whom may favor a visual learning style. Scientists also tell us processing visual images uses the right side of the brain and processing verbal/auditory information uses the left side of the brain, as Figure 2.5 shows.

They also say that we process visual images up to 400 times faster. When you use a presentation aid, the interaction between the left and right brain results in better 'whole picture' communication of your message.

3. **Audiences remember more when a visual aid is used.**

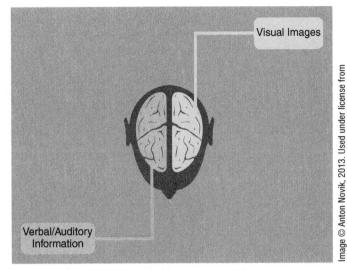

Figure 2.5 Right and Left Hemispheres of the Brain

Since the inception of television in the 1950s, each generation is becoming more visually focused and 21st century speakers must honor this increasing visual orientation. But this is good news. Studies show recall of presentation content can be increased to nearly 80 percent when the verbal information is combined with an effective visual. Indeed, people learn better with visual graphics and words rather than just words. In the study at the 3M/Wharton School at University of Pennsylvania, presentations using visual support were 43 percent more persuasive than those with no visual aids.[10] Now, in the 21st century, this visual orientation is enhanced by big screen TVs, the Internet, and visual smart phones and tablets that deliver images using high resolution and high speed graphics.

4. **Presenters using effective visuals are perceived as significantly more professional than those using only overhead transparencies.**

The research study at the 3M/Wharton School also supported the effect of visuality on professionalism:

> Communicating with the use of overhead projection will tend to influence the audience's perception of the presenter so that he'll [or she] be viewed as being better prepared, more professional, more persuasive, more credible and more interesting than those not using overheads.[11]

We hope we have made clear why *Digital Visual Literacy* is important to you as a presenter. Building on that understanding, we now turn your attention to a relatively new but related area of study called Vision Science. Understanding the theoretical foundations of Vision Science will help you create more powerful visual aids that gain and sustain the attention of your audiences.

IMAGES AND VISION SCIENCE

Vision Science is the interdisciplinary study of visual images and their role in perception. It sometimes overlaps with the study of optometry, which is more closely associated with diseases of the eye. The two areas certainly are related, but for our purposes, we are more interested in how images are processed and how they affect comprehension and perception. Hundreds of design books detail many theories related to images and their effect on people's perceptions of messages and

▼ **Vision Science**
Vision Science is the interdisciplinary study of visual images and their role in perception.

speeches. We will not take an exhaustive look at all of the theories, but rather, we will provide an overview of the three most useful notions for using images in presentations. Then we'll let you know where you can find such images.

- Pictures are Better
- Something's Missing
- Symbols Help
- Finding Good Images

Pictures Are Better

▼ **Picture Superiority Effect** suggests people remember pictures better than words

The theoretical notion of the ***Picture Superiority Effect*** suggests people remember pictures better than words. Studies do demonstrate that using images in presentations improves recognition and recall. The old saying—"A picture is worth a thousand words"—reinforces this idea. If you've ever read instructions for assembling something like a bike, you already know how important a picture can be. A picture or illustration can communicate much more information than words alone and is especially useful when conveying complex or technical information. Recall of information also is improved when words accompany an image.[12] This recall is especially true if the time lapse between exposure to the image and the recall is more than 30 seconds.

So if you want your audience to remember your presentation more than a few minutes after you've finished, try to incorporate tangible images that clearly represent your ideas. For the strongest effect in your presentation, use a concrete image as opposed to something abstract. For example, a picture of the Statue of Liberty (Figure 2.6, right slide) will be more memorable than a photo of Ellis Island (left). The aerial photograph of Ellis Island requires more processing time to understand exactly what is being depicted, but the Statue of Liberty is almost instantly recognizable.

Something's Missing

▼ **Visual Cognitive Dissonance** occurs when people see something that is incomplete or they don't understand what they are seeing

The theoretical notion of ***Visual Cognitive Dissonance*** is based on the psychological theory of Cognitive Dissonance, which says tension arises in your mind when you behave in ways that are inconsistent with or different from your beliefs.[13] You are then motivated to change either your behavior or your belief to reduce

Image © spirit of america, 2013. Used under license from Shutterstock, Inc.

Image © vetpathologist, 2013. Used under license from Shutterstock, Inc.

Figure 2.6 An Abstract vs. Concrete Image

the tension. ***Visual Cognitive Dissonance*** is a related concept that occurs when we see something that is incomplete or we don't understand. We experience a tension that we are motivated to resolve.[14] If you want your listeners to stay involved in your presentation, you can use visual dissonance to keep them engaged. You can keep them from disengaging by giving them less rather than more verbal information on your slides. Lengthy titles and lots of bullet points give away too much information and the presentation moves to a state we call "Death by PowerPoint!" The result of this approach, at best, is the audience members read the slides, and their attention wanders from your remarks. The bullet points are easily read by the audience, and in many cases, the speaker isn't even needed. There is NO tension or visual dissonance in this approach. Even in situations where speakers elaborate a little about each bullet point, it is still boring.

When you combine the concept of Visual Cognitive Dissonance with what you've learned about Picture Superiority Effect, you have a much more powerful strategy to keep your audience focused on you. When an audience is presented with an image that doesn't initially make complete sense or seems incomplete, there is conflict or tension between what they see and what they hear the speaker saying. After a first glance, the audience looks again—they want to understand what's on the screen. Audience reactions may include thoughts such as "How does this relate to her topic?", or "Where is he going with this?" You have created tension—some curiosity—and the audience feels a need to stay engaged to resolve the dissonance and find out what's going on. They will stay engaged and will look to you, the speaker, for an explanation. Their focus is on you, which is exactly what you want.

For example, let's say you are giving a history presentation. You might have a slide that lists the important dates you wish to cover (Figure 2.7, left slide). At a minimum, you should remove the busy background and add space between the lines of text. Then you can look for excess words you can remove. This would give you something similar to the slide on the right.

The redesigned slide is nice and neat, and you may have each bullet appear as you talk about it; but the slide is still dull and not very visual. Is there a better way to help your audience "see" what you're saying? A better illustration of this information? Since the information is cumulative, an animated timeline would likely be more effective.

Figure 2.8 is a much better visual presentation of the events over time and really demonstrates that you have incorporated "Visualization" into your speech development, as we recommended in Part I. Additionally, animating your timeline so

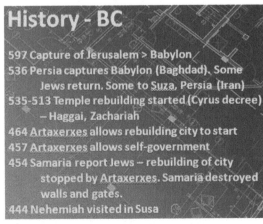

Figure 2.7 Timeline Slide Redesign

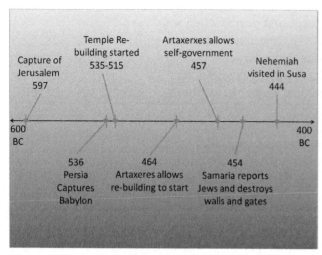

Figure 2.8 Animated Timeline

each date appears as you talk about it, your listeners will wonder what comes next.

You have accomplished two things with this illustration:

1. Kept the focus on yourself, because your audience couldn't read ahead to see where you were going with the information; and,

2. Created an expectation and a desire to continue listening to you as you complete the picture.

Not only is the visual display much more interesting, chances are, your audience will remember more of the information from your timeline than a bulleted list of dates. Of course, the timeline could be even more effective, if you could add a picture of some kind next to each new date as it appears.

Symbols Help

▼ **Iconic Representation**
Iconic Representation refers to the use of symbols or images to make information easier to remember.

The theoretical notion of *Iconic Representation* refers to the use of symbols or images to make information easier to remember. Historically, icons held religious meaning or connotations, but with the advent of computers, particularly the PC, the use of icons has flourished. One of the distinguishing features of the early Macintosh computers was the use of pictures or symbols, without text, to indicate programs or computer functions. Apple has continued this visual imagery with iPhones and iPads, and their logos are instantly recognizable worldwide. Many companies use icons to represent their brands and, in some cases, the icon is the same as the company's logo on their products or services. Icons have become prominent on the web and act as a mental "shortcut" for viewers to quickly process information about that company or product. Facebook's "Like" button or the Red Cross—which is a red cross—is instantly recognized and the viewer immediately recalls the particular product or service. (See Figure 2.9)

The author of a cleverly titled book, *Killer Presentations*, says icons in a speech or talk help us to do these four things:[15]

1. Simplify complex ideas

2. Avoid confusion

3. Speed up information transmission

4. Create visual cognitive dissonance—This approach works, if the audience questions or is not fully aware of what the icon represents.

If you want the audience to stay engaged *and* remember the key ideas in your presentation, then icons can help connect the meaning of various concepts to your words. When used properly, an icon can be a powerful visual tool in your presentation that associates a visual—nonverbal—image with your verbal message.

Images © Shutterstock, Inc.

Figure 2.9 Popular Icons

Images © Shutterstock, Inc.

Figure 2.10 Sample ISO Symbols

But remember, not all icons and their meanings are universal, so be sure to consider any potentially negative cultural inferences of the iconic image you decide to use. For example, although Facebook's "Like" button is instantly recognizable in the United States, the same symbol ("thumbs up") can signal disrespect in some middle-eastern countries. Apple Computer designers also experienced cultural differences in response to another icon they wanted to use for a specific software program. The icon was called a *moof*—a combination of moo and woof—and the icon drawing was half cow, half dog. Followers of the Hindu religion reacted negatively, because cows are considered sacred according to their religion.[16]

One way to be sure your symbols will not be considered offensive in various cultures and countries is to use symbols that have been tested and approved by the **I**nternational **S**tandards **O**rganization, known as ISO. For example, the symbols in Figure 2.10 are universally understood and safe to use in almost all situations.

Finding Good Images

The previous three sections talked about images as related to the theory of Vision Science. These are important conceptual ideas, but where can you find great images or photos? Although many software programs supply clip art as part of the package, we don't recommend using it—precisely because it has become overused and is often considered "cheesy." Those who are opposed to such cheesy images say that if Star Wars was about cheddar cheese, then some of the characters would be called the chedi's! Of course not all clip art in software programs is bad and may be appropriate in some situations. But think carefully about your audience and the speaking situation before including standard clip art in your presentation.

Whether you decide to use clip art or you need a quality photo, what are your options? It's easy to find a picture on the Internet and then "right-click" and save the picture, but there are two potential problems with acquiring pictures this way.

1. Image Resolution: Resolution of photos on the Web is usually about 72 dpi (dots per inch). If you try to enlarge the image and then project it on a screen, the image will be grainy and pixilated—the individual pixels, the small single-colored squares that comprise the image—will be visible, not very professional. This won't be a problem if you want to shrink the image, but that's not usually the case. We explain this problem more, and how to manage it, in the next section on basic design principles.

2. Copyright Laws: Capturing a screen image may violate copyright laws. Images downloaded for personal use would not be a problem, but for presentations or anything you plan to distribute, you may need copyright permission. Using a web image for educational purposes carries one set of regulations, but for a business presentation, the laws are different. Considering these restrictions, there are a number of ways to locate and legally use images and graphics in your slides. Good images can be found from stock photography websites that usually have a database where you can use keywords to search for specific

content. You can find everything from hand-drawn graphics to professional photos and videos. And learning to narrow your search by using limits such as color, size, or orientation (horizontal or vertical) can make your search more efficient and productive. These websites are specifically designed to make the permission process fairly simple. Often the permissions are listed adjacent to the photo or image you want to use.

One of the first and largest photo-sharing sites, offering over 200 million images, is www.flikr.com. Many images shown on this site carry licensing options classified as *Creative Commons*. According to the website, "Creative Commons" is a non-profit that offers an alternative to full copyright." (creativecommons.org). If you find an image you'd like to use in a presentation or handout, there are six licensing options, as specified by the "owner" of the image. Table 2.1 presents a brief description of the license types, but check the website for more specific information (www.creativecommons.org/licenses).

Several other photo-sharing sites have followed *Flikr's* example, such as *Dreamstime* (www.dreamstime.com), *iStockphoto* (iStockphoto.com), and *Shutterstock* (www .Shutterstock.com). Most of these photo-sharing sites also use categories of images that are easily searched. Licensing options for photos from these sites range from

TABLE 2.1 Attribution Licenses

Attribution CC BY	Others can use and distribute your work, even commercially, as long as they cite the source.
Attribution-ShareAlike CC BY-SA	Others can use and distribute your work, but must cite the source. Any new creation, using your original work, must also be licensed under the same terms. This is the license used by Wikipedia.
Attribution-NoDerivs CC BY-ND	Similar to the criteria above, but a user cannot change your original work in any way.
Attribution-NonCommercial CC BY-NC	Others can use and distribute your work, but not for commercial purposes. Users must still cite the source of the original work, but any new creation does not require the same license terms for a new creation.
Attribution- NonCommerical-ShareAlike CC BY-NC-SA	Others can use and distribute your work, but must cite the source, but not for commercial use. Any new creation, using your original work, must also be licensed under the same terms.
Attribution-NonCommerical-NoDerivs CC BY-NC-ND	Others can download your work, but cannot make any changes to it or use it for commercial purposes.

TABLE 2.2 Guidelines For Choosing Images And Photos

1. Make sure the image fits into the overall design scheme of your presentation. Images that vary greatly in style or color will look jarring to the audience when transitioning between slides.

2. Choose the image that meets the needs of your audience members, not just the one you like. Remember, their interpretation of the image or picture is what is important.

3. Don't choose images or photos you've seen in too many other presentations. Using images that are common to other presentations may make yours seem old or stale.

4. If you can't find exactly what you want, choose the image that is the simplest. You can always add design elements later. (More on these design elements in the next section.)

5. Finally, try to download images at 300 dpi resolution whenever possible, in order to avoid graininess and pixilation.

less than a dollar to hundreds of dollars for a single image. In addition to paying per image, many photo-sharing sites offer monthly subscriptions that allow you to download and use multiple images throughout a given month. A monthly fee may be more cost-effective, if you need more than a few images or have to create many presentations. Several other free sites also exist. The most common (as of this printing), are *Stock Exchange* (www.sxc.hu), and *PhotoBucket* (www.photobucket .com). These sites are excellent for basic photographs, but often do not have as extensive collections as the "pay-as-you-go" sites. When choosing photos or other images, keep the five guidelines in mind listed in Table 2.2.

One last note regarding images—there is a difference between free-to-use and "royalty-free." Royalty free simply means you don't have to pay every time you use it but you do pay for the rights to buy the image for use at all. If you want to keep costs down, go with the free to use option, which really means it is free. No matter what you find on the Internet, just be sure you know the specific licensing requirements for any photos you intend to use.

BASIC DESIGN PRINCIPLES

To envision information—what bright and splendid visions can result—is to work at the intersection of image, word, number, art. The instruments are those of writing and typography, of managing large data sets and statistical analysis, of line and layout and color. And the standards of quality are those derived from visual principles that tell us how to put the right mark in the right place.[17]

The author of this quotation, Edward Tufte, is a professor at Princeton University and an expert in the presentation of informational graphics, like charts and diagrams. He is a respected fellow of the American Statistical Association who coined the term "chart junk" to refer to useless, non-informative elements often found in the visual displays of information.

Getting Started by Visualizing

Vision Science theories are an important first step to understanding and effectively using visual aids in a presentation. The next step is actually designing the visuals you'd like to use. This can range from searching stock photo sites to creating something unique—like an original icon—specifically for your speech. However, before you can "design" your slides, you first have to really think about what you are trying to convey to your audience (Competency Two). You may read this statement of advice and think, "Well, duh—of course, I've thought about my main points!" But go back and think about them again (Review this section in Part I again if it might be helpful), and this time, think with pictures instead of words. As you developed the content of your speech, you used words, but inserting "visualization" into this process will only strengthen your content and your delivery.

Visualization is the representation of words or text with pictures, images, or symbols. The traditional speech creation process: choosing a topic, developing a thesis statement, researching and outlining your speech, is linear and often does not include visualization as a discrete step in developing the speech. However, it is critical to insert visualization into this process, if you want to develop a more creative and audience-focused presentation.

As we said in Part I, there is a distinct difference between "What do I need to say?" and "What does the audience need to hear . . . and see?" Reviewing the content of your presentation, using images instead of words, will help you clarify what you need as support materials and visual examples (Competency Three), and help you identify any missing information. Figure 2.12 (from Part I) provides an illustration of how visualization fits into the overall speech preparation process.

Notice in Figure 2.12 that the arrow between *Content* and *Visualization* goes in both directions. The more you think about what image will best portray your idea, the more you have to clarify your content so you can choose the correct image.

Here's an example of inserting *Visualization* into the speech development process. In a presentation about exercise, you could start with an opening slide that identifies the benefits of regular exercise, like the one in Figure 2.13.

The three main points listed on the benefits slide might provide you with talking points, but they don't do much visually for the audience. The points are a good beginning for developing your content, but thinking visually about them leads you to *images* that *illustrate* the benefits as opposed to *words* that *list* the

▼ **Visualization** refers to the representation of words or text with pictures, images, or symbols.

Image © rasskazov, 2013. Used under license from Shutterstock, Inc.

Figure 2.11 Thinking in Words

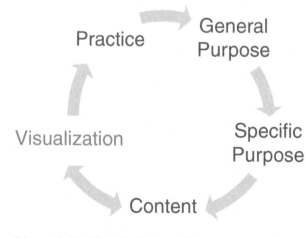

Figure 2.12 Visualization and the Public Speaking Process

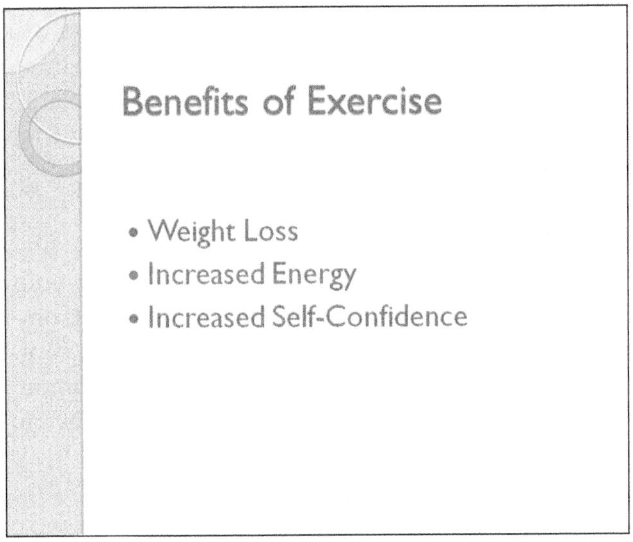

Benefits of Exercise
• Weight Loss
• Increased Energy
• Increased Self-Confidence

Figure 2.13 Opening Slide for a Presentation on Exercise Benefits

Why Exercise?

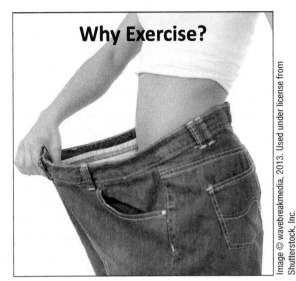

Figure 2.14 Better Opening Slide for Presentation on Exercise Benefits

benefits. As the speaker, you should say the words and let some images speak for themselves. What information are you representing with the written word that could be replaced with a photograph or illustration?

Adding this visualization step to planning the health benefits speech forces you to think about how you can visually represent the three points to your audience. Keeping in mind the fundamental concept of audience perspective, what images might appeal to your audience? Certainly if the average age of your audience is 20, your image choices likely will be different than if the average age is 50. The point is, once you insert visualization into the process you are reminded to examine your audience profile in order to come up with images that will appeal to them. The result is a more audience focused, visually stimulating presentation that will appeal to those listeners. The revised slide in Figure 2.14 offers an example of an opening image that would be more effective than a bulleted list of the three main points or benefits.

Many other types of information and data are more effectively communicated using graphics and illustrations. Figures 2.15 and 2.16 on page 31 further illustrate the idea that "one picture is worth a thousand words!" Figure 2.15 is a typical bullet point slide filled with words. Compare that with the slide in Figure 2.16, which is a better visual representation of what you're trying to convey.

Figure 2.15 answers the first question: "What do I need to say?" Figure 2.16 answers the second question: "What does the audience need to hear or see?" Figure 2.16 provides a much better visual image for the audience while you, the speaker, fill in the narrative.

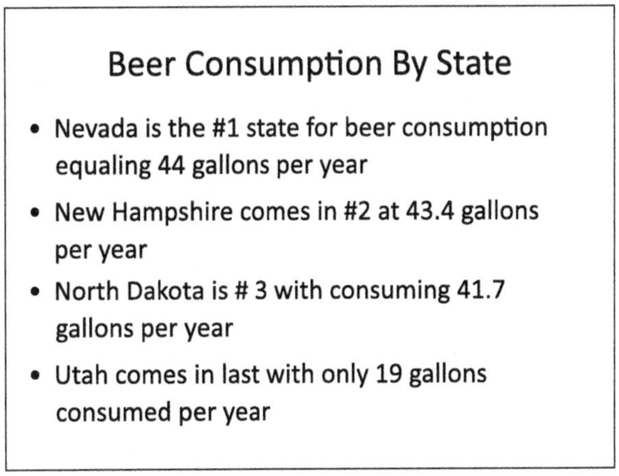

Beer Consumption By State
• Nevada is the #1 state for beer consumption equaling 44 gallons per year
• New Hampshire comes in #2 at 43.4 gallons per year
• North Dakota is # 3 with consuming 41.7 gallons per year
• Utah comes in last with only 19 gallons consumed per year

Figure 2.15 Typical Bullet Point Slide

Beer Consumption in 2011 (In Gallons)
44
43.4
41.7
19
Nevada
New Hampshire
North Dakota
Utah

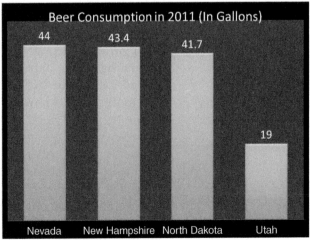

Figure 2.16 Graphic Illustration of Beer Consumption

A second benefit to using the graphic is that the audience will process what you are trying to convey much faster because the "bars" have more embedded meaning than mere words.

Inserting visualization into your speech development process is important for these four reasons:

1. Visualization enriches the early planning process for the speech.

Thinking about images and pictures that would be good representations of your ideas will help you narrow and focus your topic and content more quickly (Competencies One and Two). Determining how to visually represent your concepts helps you decide what support material to include and what to leave out (Competency Three). The sooner you decide on the content, the more time you'll have to create the actual slides and practice your presentation.

2. Visualization encourages you to keep your audience in mind.

Visualization forces you to think about how your speech will be perceived by your audience. Once you decide to use an image to communicate an idea, you must also decide if it's appropriate for the specific audience and situation. Each picture or slide should be examined in light of what you know about your audience's background and attitude toward your topic. Thinking about your audience and their reactions is the key to an effective presentation.

3. Visualization improves the overall flow and sequence of your presentation.

Thinking visually about your topic will encourage you to examine the flow and sequence of your slides (Competency Four). Presenters often just "lift" their main points off the introductory slide to make the titles on subsequent slides. This "Copy and Paste" approach doesn't encourage a thorough examination of the sequence and flow of information in the speech. Thinking about images and pictures encourages you to examine your presentation as a whole unit instead of just individual slides. As a result, you also think about the transitions you will need to move smoothly from one concept to the next.

4. Visualization of the concepts supports creative and non-linear thinking.

Developing a great presentation is not just a linear process, although many software tools and programs tend to push us into that mindset. Stepping away from the computer and really thinking pictorially and visually about your topic and its key concepts helps you use both the left and right hemispheres of your brain. Using the whole brain to develop a speech will definitely produce a better presentation than using only half of it.

Visual aids are likely to be required in most speaking situations, so it's important to understand how they can be used most effectively. Learning the underlying concepts to design better visual aids is the first step to help you become a better speaker. We encourage you to think carefully about the message you're trying to convey, and that will help you determine how to integrate visual design techniques into your next presentation. Whatever your purpose, keep your audience's needs foremost in your mind to help you create the most effective visual displays. With a better understanding of Vision Science and the role of visualization in the development of your speech, Part III outlines how to put these theoretical concepts into practice using our *SCRAP* Approach as well as other techniques for presenting data visually.

AN EXERCISE TO PRACTICE VISUALIZATION

Adding **Visualization** to your process can really enhance your content, but finding and selecting appropriate and useful photos for your presentation may prove to be more challenging than you first thought. The following activity is designed to help you practice inserting this step into the speech development process (shown in Figure 2.12).

For this activity, you (and a partner, or in a group) will go through a multi-step process to select the best picture for your topic. Each topic below is based on an abstract concept that may be interpreted in different ways based on the picture you select.

TOPICS: Freedom, Success, Racism, Morality, Friendship, Bravery, Kindness

a) Pick a topic. Define what the topic means to you and decide on your general purpose (to inform, to persuade, to commemorate).

b) Determine your specific purpose regarding this topic. What is the one central idea you'd like your audience to remember about this topic?

c) Find two images that best represent the topic. One image should be a more literal translation of the topic, and the second should be more abstract (not concrete).

   HINT: You may need to redefine/revise your concept in order to better visualize what it "looks like." For example, for the topic LOVE, the more literal translation might be a picture of two people holding hands and gazing into each others' eyes. A second image might be a big red heart.

d) Working with a partner or small group, show your *literal* image and have the other(s) guess what topic you are representing. Do the same thing with the second image.

Based on the feedback from your partner (or group members), answer the following questions.

a) Does your original image meet your intended purpose? If no, why not?

b) Did you have to redefine or clarify your concept before choosing an image?

c) Would you choose a different image after hearing the feedback from your partner or group members?

d) If you had to actually give this speech, would you use either of the images you chose? Why or why not?

e) How would this activity be different if you were discussing a more concrete topic—for example, baseball or knitting?

GLOSSARY

Data Visualization is the study of the visual representation of data.

Digital Visual Literacy is made up of two components: the ability to analyze and interpret data; and, the ability to create images to communicate messages.

Iconic Representation refers to the use of symbols or images to make information easier to remember.

Picture Superiority Effect suggests people remember pictures better than words.

Vision Science is the interdisciplinary study of visual images and their role in perception.

Visual Cognitive Dissonance occurs when people see something that is incomplete or they don't understand what they are seeing.

Visualization refers to the representation of words or text with pictures, images, or symbols.

ENDNOTES

[1] Spalter, A., & van Dam, A. (2008). Digital Visual Literacy. *Theory Into Practice*, 47(2), 93–101. doi:10.1080/00405840801992256

[2] *21st Century skills: Literacy in the digital age*. (2003). enGauge. Available online at http://www.ncrel.org/enguage.

[3] Brumberger, E. (2011). Visual literacy and the digital native: An examination of the millennial learner. *Journal of Visual Literacy*, 30(1), 19–47.

[4] Kravik, R.B. (2005). Convenience, communications, and control: How students use technology. In Oblinger, D.G., & Oblinger, J.L. (Eds.), *Educating the net generation* (p. 2.1–2.20). Educause, available online at www.educause.edu/educatingthenetgen/.

[5] Cyphert, D. (2007). Presentation Technology in the Age of Electronic Eloquence: From Visual Aid to Visual Rhetoric. *Communication Education*, 56(2), 168–192. doi:10.1080/03634520601173136

[6] Spalter, A., & van Dam, A. (2008).

[7] Oppenheim, L. (1981). *A study of the effects of the use of overhead transparencies on business meetings*. Wharton Applied Research Center, Wharton School, University of Pennsylvania.

[8] Vogel, D. R., Dickson, G. W., and Lehman, J. A. (1986). *Persuasion and the role of visual presentation support*, The UM/3M Study Management Information Systems Center, School of Management, University of Minnesota.

[9] Flemming, N., Mills, C. (1992). Not another inventory, rather a catalyst for reflection. *To Improve the Academy*, (11), 137.

[10] Vogel, Dickson, & Lehman. (1986).

[11] Oppenheim, L. (1981).

[12] Lidwell, Holden, Butler, (2010). *Universal principles of design*, Beverly, MA: Rockport Publishers, Inc.

[13] Festinger, L. (1957). *A theory of cognitive dissonance*. Evanston, IL: Row Peterson & Co.

[14] Oulton, N. (2009). *Killer Presentations*. Begboke, Oxford, UK: How to Books Ltd.

[15] Oulton. (2009).

[16] Voss, D. & Flammia, M. (2007). Ethical and Intercultural Challenges in a Shrinking Global Marketplace. *Technical Communication*, 54(1), 72–87.

[17] Tufte, E. (1990). *Envisioning information*. Cheshire, CT: Graphic Press.

Designing Presentations Using the "*SCRAP*" Approach and Other Techniques

So now you're ready to take the content you've gathered for your speech and create the actual slides that will accompany your presentation. Novice speakers simply "lift" their main points, and corresponding subpoints, and paste them onto separate slides. In an effort to add some "creativity" to the slides, beginning speakers often choose one of the templates provided with the software and select a piece of clip art to add visual interest. However, adding "visual interest" is NOT the same as applying strong visual design principles to your slides. Visual Design of your accompanying slides is part of your speech preparation (Competency Three) and is a critical skill for the 21st century speaker.

Many books are available that focus solely on the artistic elements of visual design. Of particular note is *slide:ology: The Art and Science of Creating Great Presentations.*[1] The author, Nancy Duarte, believes humans are natural storytellers. Using that concept, she works with businesses to help them incorporate visual design components into the way they tell their companies' stories. But even if you're not a trained graphic designer, like Duarte, even if you can hardly draw a straight line with a ruler, you *can* learn some basic design concepts that will help you design visually appealing speech aids. Whenever you design any kind of visual aid, you are, in fact, telling a story visually to your listeners. We now simplify this visual design process by introducing you to the five design techniques of our *SCRAP* Approach!

SIMPLIFYING VISUAL DESIGN

"A typical presenter using presentation support has nothing to lose and can be as effective as a better presenter using no visuals. The better a presenter is, however, the more one needs to use high quality visual support."

University of Minnesota/3M Study[2]

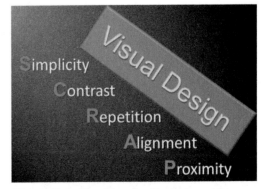

Figure 3.1 Five Simples Techniques for Effective Visual Design

The *SCRAP* Approach

▼ **The *SCRAP* Approach**
is an approach that focuses
on: *Simplicity, Contrast,
Repetition, Alignment,* and
Proximity.

Our approach to visual design, presented in Figure 3.1, emerged from a collection of ideas borrowed from many trained designers, but we have simplified them for you as a starting point for creating better visuals.[3]

Our ***SCRAP Approach*** recommends that you, as a new visual designer, make use of these five techniques: *Simplicity, Contrast, Repetition, Alignment,* and *Proximity* (Thorpe, 2012). Notice the beginning letters of these five concepts result in the acronym—SCRAP. This acronym should help you remember that much of the visualization and design process involves "throwing out" rather than "adding in." In other words, "*SCRAP* the crap!" Also, please note that these five techniques or concepts apply no matter what type of visual aid you create for a presentation: slides, posters, brochures, or handouts, literally anything. Whatever your goal, applying these principles will help you create more professional looking visual aids. We now explore each of the five design techniques in detail.

Simplicity

▼ **Simplicity**
is a design technique used to
help avoid slides that are too
busy and may overpower the
intended message.

The first technique, simplifying your slides, is where you begin. ***Simplicity*** helps you avoid slides that are too busy and overpower the message you are trying to send. In other words, "less is more." It is not necessary to put all of your "notes" on a slide. Using the slides as your personal notecards is not an audience-centered thing to do—rather, it is presenter-centered, easier for you, but not necessarily effective. Sometimes, in an effort to show how much research we have done, how much we know about a topic, or how well we can create complex graphs, we put all our data on a slide. We think this overload of information will impress the audience. Instead, such clutter overwhelms the audience and forces them to pay more attention to what's on the slide, and less attention to what you're saying. Simplicity is the essence of what one expert, Garr Reynolds, calls *presentationzen*:

> "… The kind of simplicity I am talking about does not come from a place of laziness or ignorance, rather it comes from an intelligent desire for clarity that gets to the essence of an issue, something which is not easy to do. Simplicity is not easy, in fact, it is hard."[4]

For example, if you are giving a sales presentation about bikes and want to drive home the yearly increase in sales, you might be tempted to create a slide similar to Figure 3.2. You may think this slide is dramatic and action packed, but in fact, it is too cluttered.

When determining how to simplify this slide, think about what can be deleted. What serves little to no purpose in conveying your message? You might end up with something more like the slide in Figure 3.3. You may have a hard time giving up the cool picture of bikers, but the simplicity technique says something's gotta go!

Determining what should remain on your slide and what should be deleted largely depends on your audience and your purpose (Competency Two). Giving a presentation with no bullet points is not the ultimate goal of the *Simplicity* technique. If you are creating visual aids to explain an idea or teach a concept, your slides may require more text than a presentation designed to motivate an audience, including sometimes a bulleted list. Bullet points are perfectly fine and often necessary for certain situations, but the key is careful consideration of your listeners and your purpose for speaking. Brent Dykes, author of PowerPoint Ninja Blog, explains the need for balance.

> "Just because bullet points may be perceived as the ***duct tape of PowerPoint design*** (inelegant and ugly), it doesn't mean bullet points aren't effective in certain situations. . . . . Equally important is a ***well-stocked toolbox,*** and ***knowing the right tool to use in different situations*** can be the difference between effective presentations and ineffective ones . . . ."[5]

Figure 3.2 Cluttered Slide on Bike Sales
(from Garr Reynolds, presentationzen)

Figure 3.3 Simpler Slide on Bike Sales
(from Garr Reynolds, presentationzen)

When designing slides of text and graphics, keep in mind how people read. Typically, the reader's eye is attracted to either the most brightly colored or only colored object on the page, and then it wanders back and forth between text and graphics. Using that idea, the most important object (text or graphic) should be the brightest and, if possible, should be placed in the top half of the screen. Everything else should follow a "Z" pattern below the most important thing. In the second slide about bike sales (Figure 3.3), notice how your eye or attention is grabbed by the red object and moves around from there. We call this the "Z Effect," which suggests you consider what first grabs the viewer's attention and how that attention zigs and zags away from that object.

You can understand the "Z effect" more clearly when looking at the slide shown in Figure 3.4. This slide displays four data elements in the same color, so your eye starts at the top of the slide and moves left to right, down the slide. You first note how many miles Justin biked, then Alana, and so forth down the page.

But if we change the color of one of the bars, (as in Figure 3.5) we break the Z pattern your eye would normally follow. Instead, your eye immediately focuses on the unique color bar first; then moves from top to bottom, in a left/right pattern, to view the rest of the information on the slide.

Using color to interrupt the normal "Z pattern" of eye movement, as in Figure 3.5, is particularly important when you want to highlight certain information.

Contrast

Contrast, the second *SCRAP* technique, also helps focus the audience's attention. **Contrast** refers to the differences that affect what viewers notice and what gives a design more energy.[6] Contrast comes in several forms including use of space (empty vs. filled), text sizes and fonts, and colors. Using contrasting colors (as shown previously in Figure 3.5), or even various shades of gray, can help communicate your ideas more effectively. For instance, the greater the contrast between the background and foreground colors, the easier the slide is to see and the more energetic it appears. In Figure 3.6, contrast is used to draw the eye to the main point of the slide, which is the fact that 58 percent of students' time in class is spent on texting. Fancy artwork isn't really necessary in this slide, because

▼ **Contrast**
refers to the differences that affect what viewers notice and what gives a design more energy.

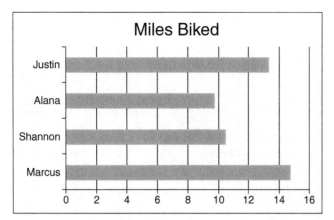

Figure 3.4 "Z Effect" Reading pattern

Figure 3.5 Using Color to alter the "Z Effect"

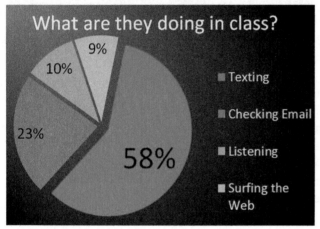

Figure 3.6 Effective Use of Color Contrast on a Slide

the contrasting colors help the audience process the information more quickly.

When visualizing and designing each slide, be certain of the slide's main point and get to that main point quickly using contrast to draw your viewer's eye to the slide's focal point. Two more examples, of weak and of strong contrast, are presented in Figure 3.7.

The top two pictures are examples of weak contrast, and the bottom two pictures illustrate strong contrast. The top two are very "busy" and present colors with little contrast. The bottom two images are simpler and use only three colors.

To better understand contrast, you also need to understand color. Colors can invoke emotional

Images © Shutterstock, Inc.

Figure 3.7 Examples of Weak (Top Slides) and Strong Contrast (Bottom Slides)

responses in your audience, some of which are based on individual experiences and others on cultural background. For example, brides in the United States wear white at a wedding and black at a funeral—so these colors may have those associations for women in the United States. By contrast, people in India wear white to a funeral and yellow is often the color of wedding dresses.

Although no concrete list of color connotations or associations is available, we can classify colors into warm and cool categories. Red, yellow, and their variations are considered warm colors, because we associate them with the sun and fire. Blue and green are cool colors, because they remind us of water and forests. The color wheel in Figure 3.8 shows the three primary colors—red, green, and blue—as well as variations or combinations of the primary colors.

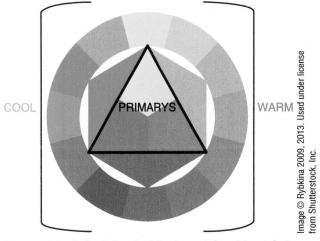

Figure 3.8 Color Wheel of Basic and Combined Colors

Color combinations, when grouped together, are called color schemes. Colors opposite one another on the color wheel are called contrasting colors and can be used to highlight or accent certain images or information. Colors next to one another on the wheel are called complementary and will work well together. Several illustrations of color schemes are presented in Figure 3.9. Note that the top, middle slide uses a monochromatic color scheme, because it includes differing hues of the same color. You can use any color scheme to achieve a desired effect, whether that effect is bold or soothing. To keep it simple, most presentation software programs offer templates or pre-designed color schemes to ensure your colors all work well together. However, it's good to understand how these schemes work, so you can choose the right one for your presentation.

This overview of contrast and color wouldn't be complete without a short explanation of how digital color works in presentations. Images displayed on a computer monitor are composed of dots, called pixels. These "pixels" can be set to different colors, using the primary colors of red, green, and blue. This RGB model is used when projecting images such as computer displays, presentations, and websites. The name of the model comes from the initials of the three primary

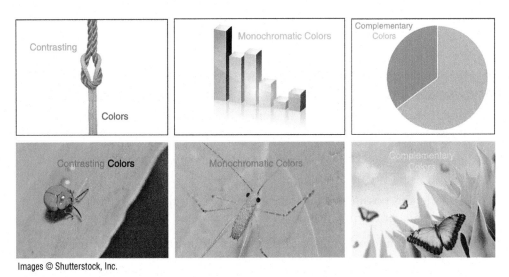

Figure 3.9 Effective Color Combinations for Slides

Figure 3.10 Pixilated Photos Lack Focus

colors—red, green, and blue. The RGB color model is an additive process in which red, green, and blue light is added together to reproduce a broad array of colors.

But have you ever found a computer image, tried to enlarge it, and noticed it seemed to lose focus? If so, you experienced what is known as "pixilation." Computer images have a resolution of 72 dpi—or dots per inch. So when you try to print or enlarge a computer image to cover a larger area, the dots or pixels must "stretch," and that causes the image to lose focus. When you're searching for images to include in your presentation, make sure the download resolution is at least 300 dpi—dots per inch. This level of resolution gives you more flexibility in case you need to enlarge the picture. To clarify this concept, two pixilated photos are presented in Figure 3.10.

Another difference between digital media and print media is the color format. Have you ever created a beautiful slide on your monitor, printed it out, and then it looked very different than when displayed on the monitor? Print media use a different color model known as the CMYK model—**C**yan, **M**agenta, **Y**ellow, and Blac**K**. These are the same colors as the ink cartridges you likely purchase for your printer. Remember: you can't just print your slides to use as handouts because when the colors are transferred to paper, they can appear very different.

By now, you may need some simple advice for choosing colors for your visual aids or slides. Table 3.1 summarizes five factors that will help you determine the best colors for your presentation, the audience, and the situation.

Repetition

▼ **Repetition** means using or reusing elements like color schemes, spacing, and fonts to bring about visual cohesion and unity in your presentation.

Technique three, **_Repetition_**, is about using or reusing elements like color schemes, spacing, layout, or fonts to bring about visual cohesion and unity in your presentation. Repetition is more than just the company logo appearing on every slide, which may just add to the clutter of information. Instead, during the visualization of your speech, did you uncover any repetitive elements? Were there any phrases or images that continually popped in your mind when you "visualized" your main points? If so, these elements could become the basis for a repetitive design that

TABLE 3.1 Determining Color Usage in Presentations

Be aware of these five factors when choosing colors for your presentation:
1. Cultural associations with color that affect how audience members may perceive your use of various colors
2. Differences in pixel display between computers and projected images that result in losing focus
3. The audience's possible color preferences based on their psychological, demographic, or cultural profile
4. The character and personality of the organization represented in the slides
5. Your personal opinions regarding colors … Just because you like pink, that does not mean it would be a good choice for a business presentation![7]

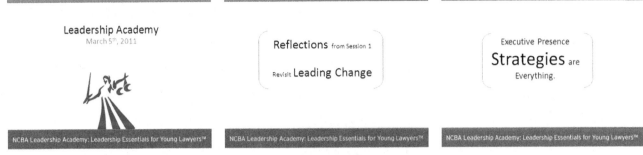

Figure 3.11 Providing Cohesion with Repetition of Layout on Slides

could be used throughout your presentation. The series of slides in Figure 3.11 provides an example of using a recurring layout to help achieve cohesion among slides. These three slides repeat the blue and grey color bars at the top and bottom of the slide as well as the font styles and colors of the text. Because the layout and color elements are repeated, these slides present a consistent design.

Many businesses and corporations try to use a consistent format for all presentation materials, so any employees responsible for presentations will present a consistent message or brand. Pre-designed templates in various software programs also help to maintain visual consistency by repeating the same message. But when overused, such repetition can become boring. So be cautious of such overuse—maintain some element of surprise.

Alignment

The fourth technique, proper *Alignment* of text and objects on the screen, helps tie elements together and make your slides look more professional. Text that isn't centered, or bullets that don't align properly, indicate a lack of attention to detail and create an unprofessional impression.

▼ **Alignment**
helps tie elements/objects together to make your slides look more professional.

When designing your slides, placement of text and objects should not look accidental or arbitrary. Each component of a slide should look as if it were positioned with intent, not just cut and pasted randomly. This alignment is equally important when only a few objects are on the screen as well as when a list of items is presented.

Alignment, as a design technique, relates closely to balance of the various elements on the slide. Not only do text and images need to be aligned properly with one another, they must be balanced on the screen as well. When you place text and images on a slide, be sure to balance the use of white or empty space with filled space. On the other hand, you don't need to have an object or some text in all four corners. Keeping in mind simplicity, just work to ensure the objects balance one another. In other words, if the screen were a plastic tray, would it tip over because of where and how you placed the objects on it? In the two slides in Figure 3.12, is the image on the left "balanced"? No, but the image on the right is.

Alignment, or rather non-alignment, also can be used to emphasize a point or image. When all other text is aligned, having one point not aligned, will immediately draw the viewer's eye to that point. This strategy can be an especially useful when transitioning between ideas or when trying to get one idea to stand out from others. An example of purposeful misalignment is shown in Figure 3.13.

Alignment can become a concern when using a numbered or bulleted list. Suppose your text takes up more than one line (which hopefully doesn't happen, for fear you break the *Simplicity* rule). Your second line may wrap around and align with the bullet or number above rather than with the text in the line above.

It Does a
Body Good

Eat more Kale

Images © Shutterstock, Inc.

Figure 3.12 Balancing Objects and Text on Slides

REPRESENTED

REPRESENTED

REPRESENTED

REPRESENTED

MISREPRESENTED

REPRESENTED

REPRESENTED

Figure 3.13 Misalignment for Emphasis on a Slide

This little piggy went to the market.
This little piggy stayed home.
This little piggy had roast beef.
This little piggy had none.

- This little piggy went to the market.
- This little piggy stayed home.
- This little piggy ate roast beef.
- This little piggy had none.

Figure 3.14 Alignment and Avoiding "Hanging Indents" on Slides

For a cleaner look, align the second line of text under the first letter in the line above. Figure 3.14 illustrates the right and wrong way to align text that continues on a second line. The second figure definitely has a cleaner look than the first. This "hanging indent" is easily fixed by manipulating the space in your software.

A final word about alignment is necessary here. When placing text on a slide, or in print media, try to avoid orphans and widows. An "orphan" is a single word appearing at the bottom of a paragraph or column. A "widow" is a word or phrase appearing at the top of a page by itself. You won't need to worry much about "widows" on a slide because most slides don't have running text. However, for handouts, "widows" can be an issue; so review any proposed handouts to make sure a single word or phrase is not on a page by itself.

Whenever possible, change the spacing or font size of your text to eliminate these problems. The two slides in Figure 3.15 show text that is limited by the size of the box. Although not a big deal, the second box looks sharper because of the elimination of an "orphan." To correct widows, insert hard page breaks that force at least two lines of text onto the next page.

- This little piggy went to the market.
- This little piggy stayed home.
- This little piggy ate roast beef.
- This little piggy ate none.

- This little piggy went to the market.
- This little piggy stayed home.
- This little piggy ate roast beef.
- This little piggy ate none.

Figure 3.15 Avoid "Orphans" on Slides

Proximity

Proximity, the fifth technique, refers to how close or far items are from one another, and it helps viewers understand "what goes with what." Proximity is a spatial concept that helps visually illustrate the relationship between objects or text. When creating slides for a presentation, many beginners like to use all of the space on a slide. They may feel uncomfortable with lots of white space, so they center the text with equal spacing among all lines. Even worse, some speakers tend to put more information on a slide than is necessary (a violation of the Simplicity technique). The result is the audience doesn't know what to look at first. Viewers then will follow the typical "Z" viewing pattern and may not be able to determine the most important thing on the slide. Remember, that through visualization, you should have determined the most important thing on the slide already. Understanding proximity will help you determine how to emphasize that important thing, what elements should be prominent, and what should be in more of a supportive role.

Using this concept when designing slides can help the audience more quickly understand the relationship of ideas in the text on the slide. The presentation is more effective because it reduces "processing time" for the audience, as they try to understand your message. They can quickly zero in on what's important. The four title slides shown in Figure 3.16 illustrate how changing the layout of the text will help your audience determine what information goes with what other information.

As you can see, the top left slide has no variation in line spacing or in font or text size. The top right slide changes the font a bit and moves and enlarges the image, but there is still no change in the proximity of the text. The bottom left slide groups lines together and adds variation in text size and font to more clearly show how the information is related. The final slide (bottom right) adds "bold" and color to the title, which indicates the relative importance of that line of text. That final slide presents an even clearer indication of "what goes with what."

▼ **Proximity**
is a spatial concept that helps visually illustrate "what goes with what."

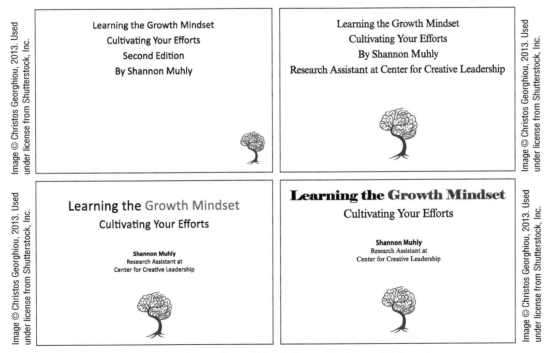

Figure 3.16 Using Proximity to Show What's Important on a Slide

Images © Shutterstock, Inc.

Figure 3.17 Using Proximity to Show Relationships Among Objects on a Slide

In addition to text, proximity also can help illustrate relationships among objects. If two or three images exemplify a specific point, place them closer together, so they will be viewed as a group. The examples in Figure 3.17 show how proximity can indicate how images are related. The left slide portrays the 3 objects as separate from one another. In the slide on the left, the use of equal distance from one another tells the viewer you will talk about them individually and equally instead of as a group. The slide on the right shows the same objects grouped more closely, which indicates there is a distinct relationship between the four objects. As the speaker, you would explain and clarify the relationship, but the audience already has a sense of this existing relationship, because of the reduced spacing between the objects. So using proximity helps your audience more quickly comprehend your meaning, and it allows them to pay more attention to you and less time to trying to understand what's on the slide.

By now you should be ready to apply the five techniques of the *SCRAP* Approach—**S**implicity, **C**ontrast, **R**epetition, **A**lignment, and **P**roximity—to your next presentation. Review our summary of the *SCRAP* techniques summarized in Table 3.2. Then we will outline two more guidelines for using *SCRAP* most effectively in your presentations—how-to's for:

(1) **Structuring text**, and

(2) **Displaying data**.

Structuring Text Effectively

One of the first things to consider when designing your slides is to determine how much text will be on a slide and how to structure that text. Too much information on a slide is one of the most common complaints of audiences. Therefore, try to cut out anything that's not necessary—remember the Simplicity principle. Be as concise as possible and avoid extra words that make a slide look busy or could be distracting to the audience.

Often public speaking students are taught about the 7/7 Rule—No more than 7 lines on a slide and no more than 7 words on each line. In reality, this may be way too much text and likely to be quite boring, particularly if each line of text starts with a bullet. The viewers will tend to read quickly through the bulleted text—the result is they won't be listening to what you say as the speaker. Now there are occasions that require bullets, like during training or in some educational settings, when the goal is primarily instructional or informative. But whenever possible, try to identify the key words in your content and then select images to represent those concepts instead of words. If your slide content does require bullet points or

TABLE 3.2 Review of *SCRAP* Technique

THE *SCRAP* TECHNIQUE	DESCRIPTION	QUESTIONS TO ASK YOURSELF
SIMPLICITY	Reduce text/objects on the slide to essential elements only	What can be eliminated that won't diminish audience understanding?
CONTRAST	Use color to highlight difference and draw the audience's attention	Can I use color to emphasize a main idea or concept?
REPETITION	Re-use colors and design elements for consistency among slides	Are there specific design elements that can (or should be) used on every slide? (Remember the Simplicity principle). Are the design elements consistent among my slides?
ALIGNMENT	Ensure text (especially bullets and lists) are properly aligned	Is title text placed (centered) properly? Are the elements balanced on the slide?
PROXIMITY	Use spacing to indicate relationship between related objects	Are the relationships between lines of text or objects immediately obvious based on the physical layout of the elements?

numbers, make sure the bullets are short phrases and not complete sentences. Or better yet, try to identify the single words that need emphasis and only put those on the slide. The top two slides in Figure 3.18 demonstrate how to simplify a bullet list into short phrases. The bottom two slides are even simpler and would allow you to cover the five bulleted ideas verbally.

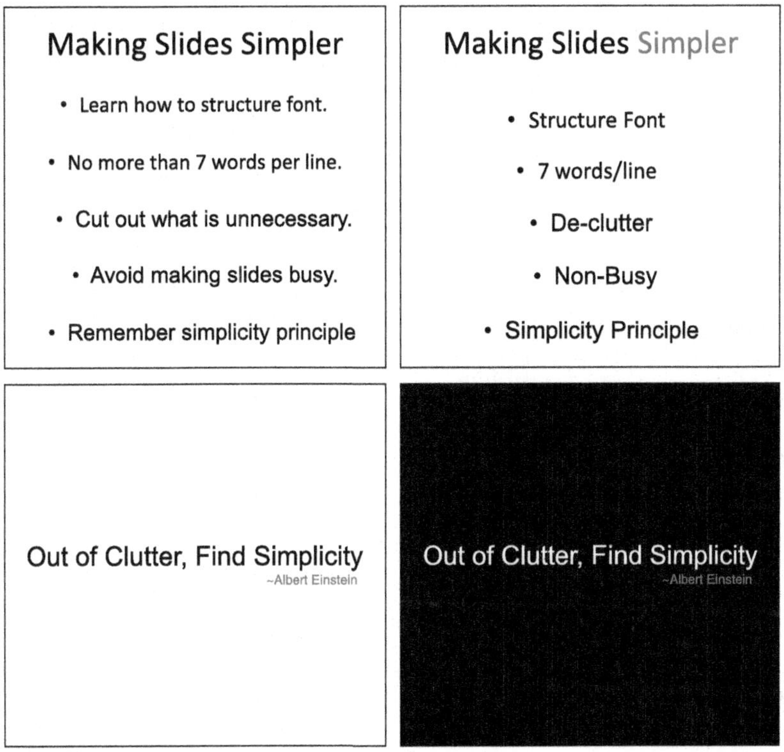

Figure 3.18 Structuring Slides for Simplicity

To really structure text effectively on slides, you also need to be aware of the following suggestions related to: keywording, parallelism, fonts, and type size.

Keywording

▼ **Keywording**
involves the process of identifying the main idea of each slide and highlighting the word(s) that support that idea.

One of the best ways to reduce the amount of text on a slide is keywording. *Keywording* refers to the process of identifying the main idea of each slide and highlighting the word(s) that support that idea. In a written essay you do this with a topic sentence and supporting material. The procedure is similar for a speech. You choose the main idea for each slide and then the important words that best illustrate that idea. Those words are the only text that actually goes on the slide. Then what you say in your spoken narrative fills in the details for the audience. Thus your slides are simple and enhance the visual and verbal content of your speech. Try this exercise to develop your keywording skills. You could try it with another student and see if the two of you come up with different main ideas and words to put on the slide.

Keywording Exercise

Identify some key text that seems to capture the meaning of the slide below (Figure 3.19). Revise the text to eliminate unnecessary words, but be sure to retain and emphasize the original meaning. This may take several restatements to pare down the text to the most essential information. Then enter the new key text or words on the blank template slide in Figure 3.20.

Parallelism

▼ **Parallelism**
is the principle of grammar having to do with consistency in wording of text on a slide to improve clearness and readability.

Simply reducing the amount of text on a slide is not enough to ensure easy reading. The structure of the phrases also should be parallel. *Parallelism* is a small but important grammatical concept used to word the text on a slide in order to improve clearness and readability. In writing, parallel structure in sentences shows how two or more thoughts are connected to one another. Bullet points on a slide also need to be parallel grammatically. Using parallel structure helps the audience recognize similar ideas and understand how the ideas are related or of similar importance.

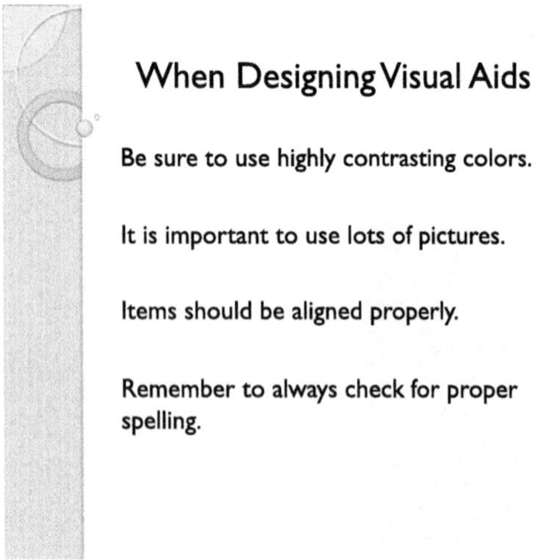

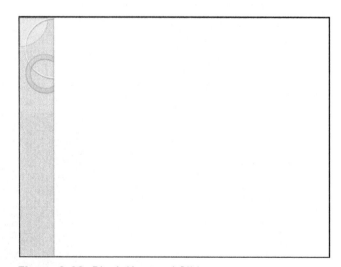

Figure 3.19 Keyword Revision Slide

Figure 3.20 Blank Keyword Slide

• Drink more water
• Read more books
• Smile and laugh more
• Family and friends are the most important things

• Drink more water
• Read more books
• Smile and laugh more
• Spend more time with family and friends

Figure 3.21 Using Parallelism on Slides

Take a moment to compare the two lists of bulleted items in Figure 3.21 and see what differences you notice. The content of both lists is the same, but the second list is parallel because all the phrases on the bullet points begin with a verb. This is a small, but distinctive way of helping the audience process your information more quickly. Such parallelism also helps make your presentation appear more professional, because of your attention to detail.

Fonts

Once you've determined the text for your slide, then you need to give some thought to the font and type size you'll use. The term *font* denotes the various digital shapes for letters and numbers that can be printed in many different sizes. Fonts can be divided into two main categories: Sans Serif (like Arial) and Serif (like Times New Roman). Sans Serif fonts are simpler in appearance and are most often used in print media like brochures, flyers, and magazines. Serif fonts have fancy-looking details on the ends of some of the strokes that make up the letters and symbols and are widely used in traditional printed material such as books and newspapers.

Indeed, some fonts are better for print materials and some are better for electronic media. Let's clarify these two types of fonts and consider which will work best for your slides.

Look at the example of Sans Serif in Figure 3.22 and note that the font does not vary between thick and thin strokes. The entire letter is the same width throughout. Common Sans Serif fonts are: Helvetica, Calibri, and Arial.

Now look at the example of Serif in Figure 3.23 and note that some of the lines of a given letter are thicker than other parts of the letter. The most popular Serif is the Times New Roman font.

▼ **Font**
denotes the various digital shapes for letters and numbers that can be printed in many different sizes.

From *Save Our Slides: PowerPoint Design that Works* by William Earnest. Copyright © 2010 by William Earnest. Reprinted by permission.

Figure 3.22 Sans Serif Font   **Figure 3.23** Serif Font

TABLE 3.3 Most Common Serif and Sans Serif Fonts

Common Serif Fonts	Common Sans Serif Fonts
Times New Roman Aa Bb Cc 1 2 3	Arial Aa Bb Cc 123
Bookman Old Style Aa Bb Cc 123	Calibri Aa Bb Cc 123
Garamond Aa Bb Cc 123	Helvetica Aa Bb Cc 123
Century Schoolbook Aa Bb Cc 123	Tahoma Aa Bb Cc 123

Table 3.3 contains a list of the most common fonts, so you can compare Sans Serif and Serif. Compare the letter "C" in both fonts. With Times New Roman (Serif), the "C" is thicker toward the middle of the letter and thinner on the ends. With Arial, the thickness of the "C" is uniform throughout the letter.

When projected on a screen in your presentation, Sans Serif fonts are more uniform and easier to read. In contrast, Serif fonts are easier to read in print materials—like in this book, which is mostly printed in a Serif font. Therefore, our recommendation is you use Sans Serif fonts on most of your slides, most of the time. In addition, try not change the type of font from one slide to the next within a presentation—that only distracts the viewers and listeners from your message.

If you need an easy way to remember the difference between Sans Serif and Serif fonts, translating the terms into French may help. The term "*Sans*" means *without* in French. Sans Serif then translates as without Serif, or without the fancy-looking details. The Serif font has the fancy stuff on letters and symbols.

Other design techniques used in print materials can be transferred to electronic media and presentations, such as using capitalization and underlining. To achieve emphasis, novice presenters sometimes display text using all capitals, assuming that makes it easier to read. Not true! The major problem with capitals is that the shape and color of the words become identical, which makes it harder to read. Using all capitals is considered "a typographic sin[8] and, in fact, reduces reading speed by 12 percent.[9] In addition, all capitals will use 30 percent more space. So remember, using capitals on all the words is not an effective way to add emphasis, nor is underlining which only clutters your slide.

Type Size

▼ Type Size
refers to how big or small the characters or symbols are—also is critical for readability.

The *size of the type*—how big or small the characters or symbols are—also is critical for readability. On any slide, a *general* rule is that the type size should not be less than 18 points, and bigger is better, particularly if you anticipate a large audience. Slide headings should be one or even two sizes larger than other text on the slide. You also can manipulate the type size for emphasis, especially numbers or statistics, if that is the main point of the particular slide. Don't be afraid to use a large font—it may look a bit overwhelming on your computer monitor, but when projected on a screen, it will be much easier to read. Some experts recommend 28 to 32 point fonts for titles and 18 to 24 for text size, but don't be afraid to use an even larger font, if it will be more effective for your purpose and audience.[10] These sizing guidelines will vary according to the font type you are using. A type size of 30 in one font may be smaller than 30 in a different font.

In addition to these guidelines for presenting text effectively, we now describe some how-to's for displaying data—statistics and numbers—in the visual design of your slides.

Displaying Data Effectively

Often, particularly in business presentations, you may need to include numerical or statistical data as part of your presentation. Statistical evidence can be very powerful support material for your topic, but only if it is well displayed. Whether you are trying to convince a group of people to buy your product, adopt a new process, or increase your project funding, the more clearly your quantitative material and data are presented, the more effective your presentation will be.

Data visualization—to be described a bit more later—is simply the study of the visual representation of data. One pioneer in this field states: ". . . graphics should reveal [not obscure] data."[11] Your audience should think "Wow, what interesting data, not "Wow, Taylor *really* went to town on that slide." Demonstrating your chart making abilities will not impress your viewers as much as choosing the most appropriate visual display to allow the data to speak for itself. Then, because the data speak clearly, you are free to talk about some non-numerical examples that bring the numbers to life for the listeners. The combination of powerful statistics and real world examples or stories makes for a powerful presentation.

▼ **Data visualization** is the study of the visual representation of data.

Many types of visual displays are available to communicate numerical information, but the key is to choose the best format for presenting your data. To illustrate how important this decision is, the first slide in Figure 3.24 shows a table of numbers that forces the viewer to figure out the relationship among the numbers. The second slide shows a line graph of the same numbers, which more clearly indicates a trend. It's obvious which visual display takes less think time for the viewer and likely would result in greater comprehension as well.

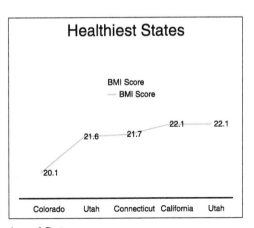

Figure 3.24 Two Approaches to Visual Display of Data

Determining which type of visual display is best for your data is based on asking these two questions:

1. What kind of data do I have? Is it numerical, categorical, geographic, hierarchical, conceptual, or what?

2. What am I trying to convey? Costs, trends, component parts, a comparison, or what?

How you answer these two questions will help you choose between the two main methods for the visual display of data: tables or figures. A *table* is a systematic arrangement of data in columns and rows. *Figures* include all other types of visual display of numbers and statistical information, other than tables. Let's look at each of these more closely.

▼ **Table**
is a systematic arrangement of data in columns and rows.

▼ **Figures**
include all other types of visual display of numbers and statistical information, other than tables.

Tables

Tables are one of the most commonly used methods for displaying quantitative or numerical information. As a result, they are often overused, or used when a different format would be a better choice. Data for a table are arranged in columns and rows, similar to a spreadsheet. Many software programs allow you to choose a table style, which standardizes the fonts and colors for your headings and helps improve readability. We should mention here that tables also are used to display text and, in those cases, are called word tables, like Table 3.3 in this book.

Tables can be a good visual choice for data related to spending or costs and can be very useful for summarizing dollar amounts. Table 3.4 illustrates such a table. However, be careful not to put too much information in a table, as it will be difficult to read and your main point may be lost. In fact, one technical communicator suggests slides with tables containing too much information are "probably the worst type of visual aid," because the audience cannot absorb all of the information presented.[12] Instead, for complex or lengthy data, the table should be included in a handout and referred to during your presentation. Then each person in the audience has their own copy to study and take home for further review.

TABLE 3.4 Displaying Data Related to Spending Costs

Bill	Amount
Water Use	$55.03
Electricity	$33.69
Gas	$39.42
Phone	$70.36
Cable	$42.25
Internet	$36.98
Car Insurance	$70.50

Here are some simple tips for using tables to present data:

- Don't put too much information in a table you intend to project on the screen.

- Use clear and simple column and row headings to help the audience categorize and understand the data with ease.

- Make sure the text size is large enough for all the data to be read effortlessly.

- If the body of your text includes dollar figures, be sure to align dollar signs and decimal points—remember about parallelism.

- Cite the source for your information at the bottom of the slide.

In sum, use tables in your presentations but use them sparingly. Too many tables are difficult to look at, and the audience may get a "glazed over" look that results from being overloaded with too much information. When deciding whether to use a table or not, think first about keywording—discussed earlier—to see if there is another way to present your data that is more creative and possibly more effective.

Figures

Figures include any visual display that does not have columns and rows. The term figure includes line graphs, bar charts, pie charts, flowcharts, diagrams, and maps, and any combination of these forms.

Line graphs are useful for any data that indicates a trend in data over time, whether a flat trend—no change—or a positive or negative trend. The line or lines on the graph often are drawn chronologically. A line graph is composed of an x and y axis. The x axis (horizontal) usually shows the progression over time and the y axis (vertical) usually indicates the thing being measured. Line graphs can display more than one line in order to compare trends across categories or regions. Figure 3.25 shows yearly sales figures for XYZ company's three regional offices using colored lines to indicate each of the three offices.

Surface charts are a specific form of the line graph, but the data are cumulative. You can think of a surface chart as similar to adding colored sand to a jar. As you add the different colors, you can clearly see the individual colors even as the total amount of sand increases. If you have data that "accumulates," you could use a surface chart to depict the contribution of each component, yet still illustrate how they contribute to the total. If you decide to use a surface chart, be sure to place the largest contributor or segment at the bottom. Figure 3.26 visually illustrates data displayed on a surface chart.

Bar charts are very versatile and work well when you require a side-by-side comparison of data. The height of the bars illustrates the data and provides an efficient visual display to help the audience quickly understand numbers and their meaning and relationship. The side-by-side comparison can be horizontal or vertical depending on your x axis and y axis and which bar you want to emphasize. Figure 3.27 displays data using a vertical bar chart and Figure 3.28 uses a horizontal bar chart.

Using color to contrast the different bars in the chart is a great way to draw the viewers' attention to the comparisons you are making. You also can use color as a contrast to draw the audience's eye to a main point you want to highlight in the data. The vertical bar chart in Figure 3.27 uses color to show how much more money was made from garage sales (red) than washing cars or mowing lawns (blue). Not only is the height of the middle bar significant, but color is used to magnify

▼ **Line graphs**
are useful for any data that indicates a trend in data over time, whether a flat trend—no change—or a positive or negative trend.

▼ **Surface charts**
are a specific form of the line graph, but the data are cumulative.

▼ **Bar charts**
are very versatile and work well when you require a side-by-side comparison of data.

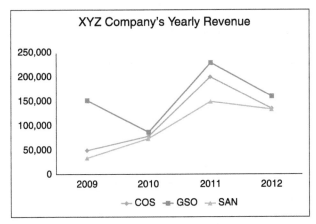

Figure 3.25 Effective Line Graph

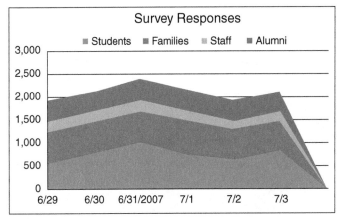

Figure 3.26 Effective Surface Chart

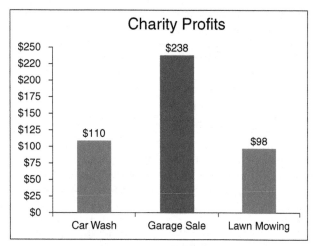

Figure 3.27 Effective Vertical Bar Chart

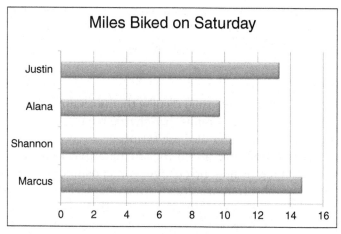

Figure 3.28 Effective Horizontal Bar Chart

this contrast. But although color is very useful for contrast on slides, if you are printing black and white handouts, this same contrast will not be obvious. Consider using shades of grey to black to provide some degree of contrast among the bars.

As with tables and line graphs, do not put too many bars on one graph. Overloading the slide dilutes the impact of your data and forces the explanatory text and legend on the slide to be smaller. If you have more than six bars for any one chart, consider whether you can split the chart in some way and use multiple bar graphs to display your data.

A *pie chart* often is used for displaying a part of something as it relates to the whole thing. Pie charts are simple, but very effective, when used with the appropriate data. For example, using a pie chart to represent sales growth would not be the best visual choice. However, a pie chart to indicate specifically where the growth comes from would be a perfect fit. In other words, if you want to highlight a portion of something, if one division was the major contributor to overall sales growth, then a pie chart is the right visual display format. The pie chart in Figure 3.29 clearly and simply shows that research efforts account for 35 percent of the company's profits.

If you use a pie chart, try to keep the number of slices in the pie at six or below to maximize the visual impact. If you have too many pie slices, the audience is forced to read too many data labels on the pie slices. In such a case, a table may be a better visual choice. A pie chart is really best for instant visual impact, not for data that requires comparison or calculation. Another technique to add this visual impact is to "remove" one slice and move it away from the rest of the pie, often referred to as "exploding the pie." Figure 3.29 uses this technique to call attention to the research slice of the pie. Finally, be sure to accurately label each pie slice and enlarge the type size to make the data easier to see. Ideally, labels should be inside the pie slices, as long as the text is still easily read.

A *flowchart* is an illustration of a sequence from beginning to end. Showing a process, or a decision tree, are both good examples of when to use a flowchart. When you create a flowchart, the shapes of the objects are not as important as ensuring you use the

▼ **Pie chart**
often is used for displaying a part of something as it relates to the whole thing.

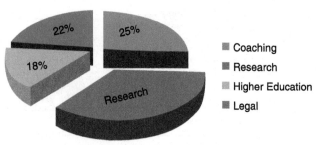

Figure 3.29 Effective Use of "Exploding the Pie"

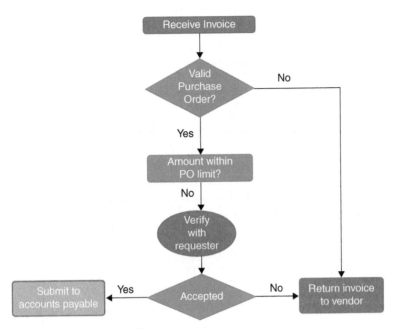

Figure 3.30 Effective Flowchart

shapes consistently and correctly. Figure 3.30 shows a typical flow chart for making a decision about submitting an expense report.

Although flowcharts can be very useful to visually depict a process, make sure you are clear about your specific purpose. If the flowchart is intended to explain a process, think about animating the shapes to appear as you introduce each step in the process. Then your audience will be able to follow the process as you describe it, and you won't reveal too much information too soon. Or if you want to use a flowchart to highlight a specific step in the process (as opposed to the sequence of the process), use a bright color to help that step stand out from others in the process.

An *organization chart* is helpful when you're trying to show relationships among people or departments. Providing a chart depicting the structure of an organization can help the audience envision how communication networks flow or interrelated jobs work together. The suggestions for creating flow charts also apply to organization charts—think about what you want to emphasize and use visual design and color to draw attention to that point.

▼ **An Organization chart** is useful when you're trying to show the relationship among people or departments.

The phrase "A picture is worth a thousand words"—that we used several times already—certainly applies to the need for a good *diagram*, which is a pictorial aid to understanding. If you've ever found yourself trying to assemble something and becoming frustrated, you know the value of a diagram. Whenever a presentation includes explaining how to do something, then you will likely need a diagram to help your audience understand your instructions more quickly.

▼ **A Diagram** which is a pictorial aid to understanding.

Depending on the topic, some diagrams may be too complex to present in their entirety on a slide, so you need to simplify the diagram. Gurak, author of a book on technical presentations, suggests you "isolate out one portion of the diagram, enlarge it, and use just that part."[13] The complete diagram, if it is really needed, can be included in a handout. Figure 3.31 illustrates the pathway of blood through the heart, but the labels are quite small, so this diagram may be better suited for a handout.

Maps and geographic data can be used when trying to show locations, distance, points of interest, or the geographic distribution of data, such as regional sales, or voter registration by state. Geographic Information Systems is a growing

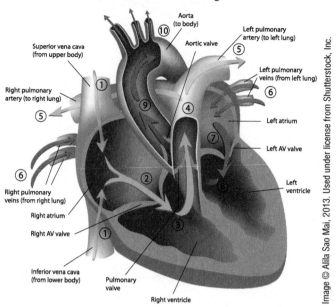

The pathway of blood flow through the heart

Figure 3.31 Diagram Better Suited for a Handout

field that uses aerial or satellite imagery to analyze and display various types of data. You may use some sort of mapping device for driving directions, to find the closest gas station, or to determine how far your hotel is from the airport. These are only a few examples of how geographic information and data are becoming integrated into our everyday lives.

For presentations, we need to use geographic data whenever it will help an audience visualize how things are spatially related. For example, a speaker trying to convince an audience to install Wi-Fi in a business could show Table 3.5 on the next page that lists the addresses of all the competing businesses within a five-mile radius with Wi-Fi.

However, given this speaker's purpose, a better visual display would be a map of the nearby competitors who already have Wi-Fi. The map in Figure 3.32 on the next page is certainly more impactful than a list of the competitors' names and addresses, and the audience won't need to study and interpret the data from the table.

TABLE 3.5 Nearby Competitors with Wi-Fi

Tire Places	Locations	Wi Fi
1) Company A	707 S 8th St	No
2) Company B	220 S Chestnut St Unit B	No
3) Company C	509 W Colorado Ave	Yes
4) Company D	509 S Nevada Ave	Yes
5) Company E	770 Abbot Ln	No
7) Company F	1117 S Nevada Ave	No
8) Company G	1611 S Nevada Ave	Yes

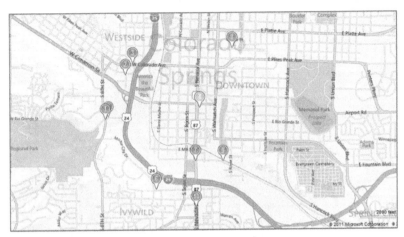

Figure 3.32 Map of Nearby Competitors with Wi-Fi

Data Visualization

Almost everything we talked about in Part II, including the visual design principles, relates to the visual display of data. However, Data Visualization has an even more expansive meaning. There are various definitions but, in general, **_Data Visualization_** refers to "any technology that allows or aids any . . . end users to 'see' data in order to help them better understand the information and put it in context." (http://searchbusinessanalytics.techtarget.com/). Data Visualization can combine the types of visual display just discussed—like tables and figures—but with the goal of displaying broad meaning rather than individual data points. It is more important to show the broader context of meaning rather than specific detail. In other words, learning to *visualize* data helps provide context to sets of numbers. According to Ben Shneideman, founding director of the Human-Computer Interaction Laboratory at the University of Maryland, "The purpose of visualization is insight, not pictures."[14]

Various applications and websites are available to help you create dynamic visualizations of data that go beyond line graphs and bar charts. An early pioneer in the field of data visualization is Dr. Hans Rosling, a professor of Global Health, at Korlinska Institute in Sweden. Dr. Rosling studies world health issues, such as AIDS, poverty, birth rates, and more. To help his audiences **see** his data as opposed to just reading it, he developed software called *Trendalyzer*. With this tool (now owned by Google), users can convert statistics into moving, interactive graphs, which are far more powerful than a table of numbers. To see videos of his presentations using this software, go to www.gapminder.org/.

Figure 3.33 provides another example of an advanced data visualization display.

This image was taken by Marc Smith, a social media researcher. This graphic depicts the connections among the Twitter users who tweeted the word *educon* on January 26, 2012. Connections were created when users replied, mentioned, or followed one another. The underlying data in the graphic was generated using NodeXL software (Network Overview Discovery and Exploration for Excel 2007/2010) and is an open source product from the Social Media Research Foundation (http://www.smrfoundation.org/), a collaborative effort involving many partners. This software generates maps from social media network data and can provide insightful analysis and visualization of social media covnnections.

Although it may seem as if you need to be a computer science major to produce highly visual images that is not the case. As long as you have a basic understanding

▼ **Data Visualization** refers to "any technology that allows or aids any . . . end users to 'see' data in order to help them better understand the information and put it in context."

© Lefteris Pitarakis/AP/Corbis

Rosling presenting 200 years, 200 countries, 4 minutes http://www.youtube .com/watch?v=jbkSRLYSojo

Twitter social media map of "Educon" tweets created by NodeXL by Marc A. Smith, 2012. http://www.flickr .com/photos/marc_smith/6785112263

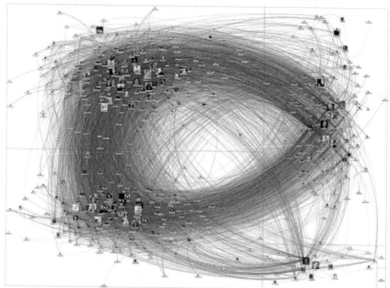

of how to input data into a spreadsheet, you can begin to create visual images from large data sets. The point is, as the level of information and data increase, so does the need for public speakers to convert numbers into something more visual. The goal is to use visuality to help your audience really understand the important pattern or trend you are trying to present, instead of getting lost in a mass of numbers. When you are ready to try this technique, review *22 free tools for data visualization and analysis* from ComputerWorld magazine to help get you started[15] (http://www.computerworld.com/s/article/9215504/22_free_tools_for_data_ visualization_and_analysis).

INTEGRATING BIG IDEAS FROM PARTS II AND III

▼ *SCRAP*
focuses on: Simplicity, Contrast, Repetition, Alignment, and Proximity

Part II of this book started with a discussion of Digital Visual Literacy and some theoretical ideas we borrowed from the field of Vision Science. In Part III, you learned some basic design techniques, including the *SCRAP* Approach that focuses on: *Simplicity*, *Contrast*, *Repetition*, *Alignment*, and *Proximity*. Figure 3.34 provides a summary of the main ideas from Parts II and III.

Hopefully, Part II and III have significantly expanded your understanding of the competencies presented in Part One:

Narrowing your Topic—Competency One
Defining your speech purpose—Competency Two
Gathering support materials—Competency Three
Organizing your content—Competency Four

If you follow the first four competencies presented in Part I, practice the visualization steps outlined in Part II, and use the basic design techniques and guidelines provided Part III, then you're ready to move to the next step in developing an effective presentation. Part IV provides instructions and ideas for using today's most popular digital presentation tools—like *PowerPoint* and *Prezi*. But first, to fully integrate what you have learned in Parts II and III, you may want to try your hand at redesigning some visual aids based using the following exercise.

What is Digital Visual Literacy?

Why is it important?

Is it worth the effort?

Digital
Visual
Literacy

Vision
Science

Pictures are Better

Something's Missing

Symbols Help

Finding Good Images

Basic
Design
Techniques

SCRAP Approach

Structuring Text

Displaying Data Effectively

Figure 3.34 Integrating the Ideas

VISUAL AID REDESIGN EXERCISE

This exercise gives you the opportunity to redesign two slides in a way that adheres to good design principles. Look at Slides #1 and #2 and start by visualizing the main idea the slide is trying to convey.

Slide #1

Crow Pose

1. Bending the knees slightly, bring your palms flat on the floor about shoulder distance apart.

2. Place the knees on the back of the upper arms.

3. Start to come forward, lifting the head as you go.

4. Take feet off the floor, one at a time, so you come to balance with both feet up.

Slide #2

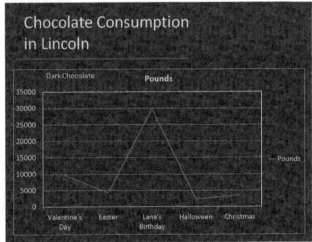

1. Using the *SCRAP* techniques you learned in this section, identify the specific areas that need improvement.

2. Sketch or describe what you think a new slide should look like.

3. Compare your ideas to the revisions of the slides that we present below.

4. What principles and techniques did we apply to the redesign of the slides? What principles did you apply?

Slide #1

Slide #2

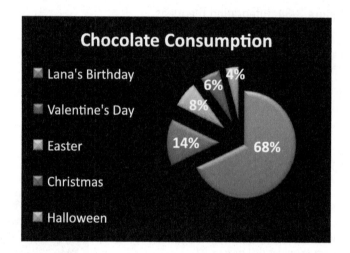

2. In the slide below, identify 7 specific design and content problems. Once you've come up with your list, compare it with the slides below.

Slide #3

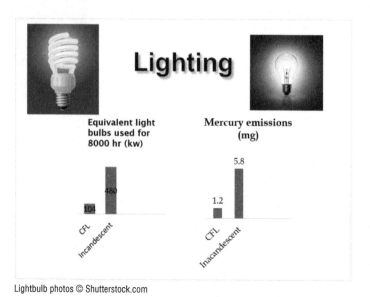

Lightbulb photos © Shutterstock.com

Slide #4   ## Slide #5

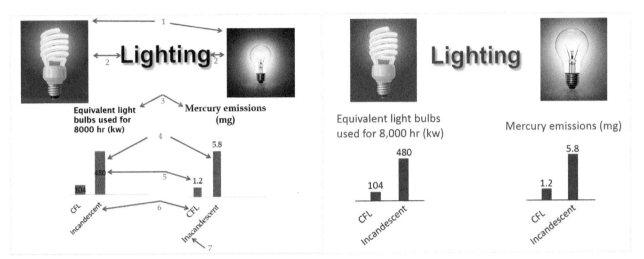

Lightbulb photos © Shutterstock.com

Slide #4 indicates the *SCRAP* and content issues that should be addressed.

a. Images are unequal sizes (Repetition and Alignment)

b. *Lighting* is not centered properly between the 2 images (Alignment)

c. Image titles are not aligned (or clearly associated) with the images, nor do they use the same font (Repetition, Alignment, Proximity). Also, notice the "orphan" (mg).

d. Bars are not the same height and width (Repetition)

e. Text does not use the same font (Repetition)

f. Labels are not in the same position (Repetition)

g. *Inacandescent* is spelled incorrectly—not a design issue, but certainly a critical mistake

The slide on the right (Slide #5) shows what the slide would look like after correction. Simple, yes, but much more effective.

Each of these design issues is easy to fix, and when completed, combine to display a cleaner, more professional looking slide. As you prepare your slides, remember to go through the *SCRAP* principles to determine if you have applied them to all components of your visual aids.

GLOSSARY

Alignment helps tie elements/objects together to make your slides look more professional.

Bar charts are very versatile and work well when you require a side-by-side comparison of data.

Contrast refers to the differences that affect what viewers notice and what gives a design more energy.

Data visualization is simply the study of the visual representation of data.

A Diagram is a pictorial aid to understanding.

Exploding a pie slice is a technique used to add visual impact to a pie chart by separating one slice and move it away from the rest of the pie.

Figures include all other types of visual display of numbers and statistical information, other than tables.

A Flowchart is an illustration of a sequence from beginning to end.

A Font is the digital shape for letters and numbers that can be printed in many different sizes.

Graphs can be used for any data that indicates a trend in data over time, whether a flat trend—no change—or a positive or negative trend.

Keywording involves the process of identifying the main idea of each slide and highlighting the word(s) that support that idea.

Line graphs are useful for any data that indicates a trend in data over time, whether a flat trend—no change—or a positive or negative trend.

An Organization chart is useful when you're trying to show the relationship among people or departments.

Parallelism is the principle of grammar having to do with consistency in wording of text on a slide to improve clearness and readability.

A Pie chart is often used for displaying a part of something as it relates to the whole thing.

Proximity is a spatial concept that helps visually illustrate "what goes with what."

Repetition means using or reusing elements like color schemes, spacing, and fonts to bring about visual cohesion and unity in your presentation.

The SCRAP Approach is an approach that focuses on: *Simplicity*, *Contrast*, *Repetition*, *Alignment*, and *Proximity*.

Simplicity is a design technique used to help avoid slides that are too busy and may overpower the intended message.

Type size refers to how big or small the characters or symbols are and is critical for readability.

Surface charts are a specific form of the line graph, but the data are cumulative.

A Table is a systematic arrangement of data in columns and rows.

ENDNOTES

[1] Duarte, N. (2008). *Slide:ology: The art and science of creating great presentations*. Sebastapol, CA: O'Reilly Media.

[2] Vogel, D. R., Dickson O. W., & Lehman J. A. (1986). *Persuasion and the Role of Visual Presentation Support: The UM/3M Study*. Retrieved from: http://www.thinktwiceinc.com/olio/articles/persuasion_article.pdf

[3] Williams, R. (2010), *The non-designer's presentation book: Principles for effective presentation design*. Berkeley, CA: Peachpit Press.

[4] Reynolds, G. (2008). *presentationzen: Simple ideas on presentation design and delivery*. Berkeley, CA: New Riders.

[5] Dykes, B. (2009, January 10). *PowerPoint Design in 2009: A Hammer or a Toolbox?* Retrieved from http://www.powerpointninja.com/philosophy/powerpoint-design-in-2009-a-hammer-or-a-toolbox/.

[6] Reynolds, G. (2008). *presentationzen: Simple ideas on presentation design and delivery*. Berkeley, CA: New Riders.

[7] Arnston, A. (2007). *Graphic design basics*. Belmont, CA: Thomson Wadsworth.

[8] Endersby J. (1993). *All caps: a typographic sin* Desktop 71 (July): 72–73.

[9] Marcus, A. (1992). *Graphic Design for Electronic Documents and User Interfaces*. New York, NY: ACM Press.

[10] Munter, M. and Paradi, D. (2012). *Guide to PowerPoint version 2010*. Upper Saddle River, NJ: Pearson Education, Inc.

[11] Tufte, E. (2001). *The visual display of quantitative information*. Cheshire, CT: Graphic Press.

[12] Hay-Roe 1999. p. 23

[13] Gurak, L.J. (2000). *Oral presentations for technical communication. 1st ed.* Boston, MA: Allyn and Bacon.

[14] Singer, N. (2011, April 2). When the Data Struts its Stuff. *New York Times*. Retrieved from http://www.nytimes.com/2011/04/03/business/03stream.html?_r=1&emc=eta1.

[15] Machlis, S. (2011, April 20). *22 free tools for data visualization and analysis*. Retrieved January 20, 2013, from www.computerwold.com: http://www.computerworld.com/s/article/9215504/22_free_tools_for_data_visualization_and_analysis

Building Presentations in the 21ˢᵗ Century

After you develop the content for your presentation, you can use one of several popular software programs to bring your concepts to life. Many such programs are available, and many more are in development all the time. In this part of our book, we discuss the two most common software packages used to develop visual aids for a presentation—PowerPoint (2013) and Prezi.

This Part IV is not meant to be a beginners' tutorial for learning to use a specific software program. Other books and videos already exist to teach you the basics of using these two programs, and most of the embedded training materials accompanying them are intuitive and easy to follow.

Rather, this section is intended to help you *digitally apply* the visual design principles and concepts covered in Parts II and III to the development of your speech. No matter how much thought and preparation you put into developing your content, it won't matter if you can't "translate" that to a visually appealing format for your intended audience.

Most audience complaints about presentations focus on how the speakers visually display information, which suggests these speakers didn't read our book! Figure 4.1 is one possible result. Clearly, how you visually portray your thoughts will significantly impact your credibility with the audience (not to mention your speech grade).

Deciding whether to use PPT or Prezi is up to you as each program has advantages and disadvantages. PowerPoint is very good for presenting linear, factual information and offers a variety of ways to display data. Therefore it may work well for an informative speech, as described in Part I. It allows you to insert images, video, and audio and manipulate these files within the PPT environment. In addition, most businesses use PowerPoint, which means it's highly likely that your peers

Andrey_Popov/Shutterstock.com

Figure 4.1 The Result of a Boring Visual Display!

and colleagues can easily make changes and updates to your presentation without learning new software. These same features are also the disadvantages in that people associate PowerPoint with dull, boring bullet points.

Prezi, on the other hand, begins with a "blank canvas" and offers much more freedom and flexibility for the flow of your material. If you need more detail about a certain topic, you can "Zoom" in on that material, or skip it altogether, depending on your audience. However, as with PowerPoint, an advantage can quickly become a disadvantage, if the slides are still boring bullet points or the speaker uses the Zoom feature to distraction. After reading Parts I through III, you already know these are "operator-error" issues, and not a problem with the software. Learning the basics of visual design and the various features of your software tools are the keys to a visually interesting presentation.

We fully recognize that you can get this kind of step-by-step user information online, while simultaneously building your slides, so why include this chapter on how to use the software? Having viewed literally thousands of speeches and presentations (between the two of us), we have seen that students often "don't know what they don't know." In other words, most presenters are never really taught advanced features of a software program, so they couldn't possibly know what the software is capable of. If you don't have any idea of what the tool can do, how could you begin to "search" for good advice online? That's why we included this part of the book.

We wanted to highlight very specific features of these software tools that are misunderstood, underused, used poorly, or not used at all. Learning to use these special features, based on the design principles outlined in Parts II and III, will set your presentations apart from all others.

Throughout this discussion, we offer several tips to highlight the most common mistakes speakers make when building their slides. These tips are easily identified by the Quick Tip icon—and they apply no matter what presentation software you may be using. We show both *Before* and *After* images so you can clearly see how adhering to the *SCRAP* principles will help you build better visual aids.

We begin with PowerPoint, because more than 90 percent of all presentations use it. However, just because it is commonly used, that does NOT mean that most of us use PowerPoint very effectively. The popular phrase, "Death by PowerPoint," clearly indicates we have some work to do in order to use this software tool most successfully. After a detailed discussion of using PowerPoint, then we'll provide a description of Prezi, including suggestions for using both of the programs well.

BUILDING PRESENTATIONS WITH POWERPOINT

For simplicity, and because you likely have some familiarity with PowerPoint (PPT), our coverage is presented in the order of the steps you're likely to follow to create slides for your presentation. Our approach is to use several of the visuals presented in Parts II and III and show you how to create them for yourself. Once you become familiar with the tools for one slide, you will find it easy to use the same features to create any slides you need for any presentation.

We will not cover every possible feature or function, but we will highlight those most commonly underused, or those most people don't know how to use well. As we explain each of these features, we will relate them (whenever possible) to the design principles you learned in Part II.

Ideally, you will have followed the guidelines for the first four competencies presented in Part I through Part III, before you even sit in front of a computer to build your slides. If so, actually building your slides will be easier and faster. However, if you haven't fully developed your purpose, or thought about how you will visually support your concepts and organize your material, you should give those steps further consideration before moving on.

Once you're ready to build the slides, we offer the following six simple steps to get started (Table 4.1). Although you can approach the physical creation of your slides in any order, we suggest this sequence, because it fosters a solid design foundation to which you can add an unlimited number of visual components.

TABLE 4.1 Slide Build Sequence

1. Creating Basic Slides

2. Inserting Pictures and Objects

3. Enhancing Slides

4. Building Tables and Figures

5. Adding Animation

6. Generating your Slide Show

1. Creating Basic Slides

Before you begin creating your individual slides, you need to give some thought as to whether you'll use a *Slide Master*. A *Slide Master* is a slide that helps to maintain continuity across all of your slides by establishing positions for objects on the slides, and color and font choices. A *Slide Master* is very useful for consistency in your design elements, and it saves you time by not having to add individual elements, such as the slide number, to every slide. Items in the *Slide Master* will appear on all slides so it's best to establish a *Slide Master* before creating any other slides.

Edit the Slide Master

1. From the *View* tab -> Select Slide *Master* (Figure 4.2)

   This will bring up this *Slide Master* Tool Bar (Figure 4.3) and a slide with existing design elements.

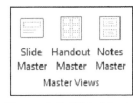

Figure 4.2 Slide Master

Figure 4.3 Slide Master Toolbar

From this screen you can:

■ Add place holders for new objects (text, pictures, tables, etc.) (To delete objects you don't want, simply select the object and press the *Delete* key)

■ Edit the presentation theme

- Change font style (be sure to select a Sans Serif font)
- Determine slide colors
- Change the slide background
- Change the size of your slides (particularly useful if you're displaying the presentation on a laptop with a widescreen).

PowerPoint also offers "ready-made" design themes, called *Templates*. *Templates* establish all of the design elements for you. Templates include object positioning, font and color choices, as well as various patterned backgrounds. Although this may sound like an easy solution to your consistency issues, we recommend against using these popular templates whenever possible. Earlier versions of PowerPoint (2003, 2007, 2010) often incorporated many extraneous design elements, such as distracting graphics, or patterned backgrounds, that didn't add anything to a presentation and likely even distracted from your intended message. PowerPoint 2013 has attempted to rectify this problem a bit and now offers thousands of templates in many different categories for you to choose from. These newer templates are certainly better, but they still constrain you to a structure that may not be best suited for your content. You can use these templates as a starting point or design your own using the *Slide Master*. In either case, be sure to follow the *SCRAP* approach outlined in Part III.

Once you have created your *Slide Master*, you can begin to build the individual slides for your presentation. In Part I, we encouraged you to visualize your slide content (supporting material). However, even if most of your slide content will be an image, it is likely you'll still need a few slides with text, like an opening slide, so we'll talk now about editing a text box (You probably already know this, but it's a good starting point).

Edit a Text Box

When you open a new presentation, you are asked to choose a *Slide Layout* format. PowerPoint offers various slide formats with placeholders for text boxes, images, or tables already positioned on the slide for you.

Pre-designed layouts are convenient for title slides, or slides with several bullet points, but as with templates, don't rely on these too much.

It is very easy to just click in the text box and begin typing your content. However, you may have noticed that PPT likes to fit the text to the size of box provided, and this can be very annoying when you are trying to keep the type size as large as possible.

Therefore, the best thing to do is . . .

Turn off the Autofit feature.

1. Right-click on the border of the text box.

2. Select *Format Shape* at the bottom and the dialog box will appear.

3. Select the *Size and Properties* icon and *Text Box* Options will appear. (Figure 4.4)

4. Select *Do not Autofit*.

Once you've turned off *Autofit*, PPT will not automatically resize your text to fit the size of the text box. However, if your text size is large, you may need to enlarge the text box to see all of the words or letters.

▼ **Templates**
are a series of slides in which all of the design elements are established for you, including object positioning, font and color choices as well as various patterned backgrounds.

Figure 4.4 Text Options

Even if you have nothing but bullet points, enlarge the font as much as possible (minimum 28 pt.), add color (*Contrast*) and increase line spacing (*Proximity*) to create a slide that's easier to read.

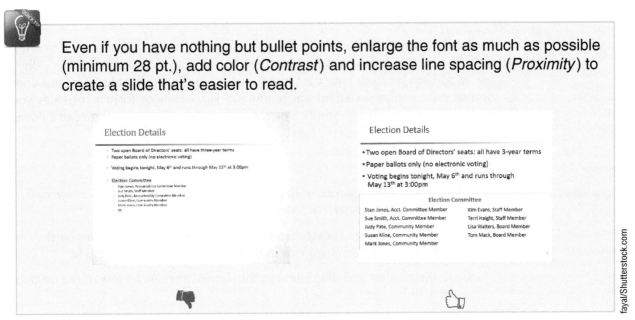

Figure 4.5 Before and After Bullet points

2. Inserting Pictures and Objects

Adding and editing text boxes is simple, but as you learned in Part II, too much text usually means dull and boring slides. To communicate your ideas better, you need something more visual—pictures or images—or some other enhancement. All of these additions are called objects and are treated similarly. When deciding whether to use an image or clip art, remember the concepts covered in Part II about image quality and copyright laws.

No matter what you need to insert, you will start from the *Insert* toolbar, which looks like Figure 4.6.

Figure 4.6 Insert Toolbar

As you can see from the lower portion of this toolbar, PowerPoint contains these nine categories for inserting things into your presentation:

- Slides
- Tables
- Images
- Illustrations
- Links
- Comments
- Text
- Symbols
- Media

At some point, you may use all of these tools but, for now, we provide some general guidelines and how-to's that apply mostly to inserting and using: *Tables, Images, Illustrations, Links, and Media.*

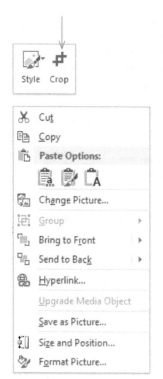

Format a Shape

You've probably already created slides that included an image, or some clip art, so we'll assume you know the basics of inserting an image. PowerPoint 2013 allows you to add images from your computer or search online for images. The real question is, once you've added an image, do you know how to format it to suit your particular purpose? For example, you might have found a great picture of a flower, but want to crop it to remove surrounding objects.

To crop a picture:

1. Right-click on the border of the image. This will bring up the *Picture Tools* toolbar at the top as well as a shortcuts menu on your slide.

2. Select *Crop* from the Shortcuts menu and you will see the handles (at the corners) of the image change to indicate that you are in *Crop* mode.

3. Grab the handles and drag them to the desired size. A shadow of the original image will remain underneath.

4. Right-click on the slide, away from your image, and your changes will be saved on the slide.

Figure 4.7 Crop an Image

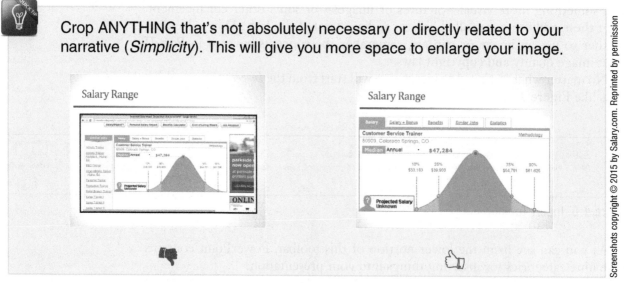

Crop ANYTHING that's not absolutely necessary or directly related to your narrative (*Simplicity*). This will give you more space to enlarge your image.

Figure 4.8 Before and After Cropping – Authors slides, but image came from Monster.com website

Insert a Screenshot

Suppose you need a picture of something in your presentation from your computer screen. For example, in training courses, the presenter often needs a picture of the screen as it looks when completing a certain task. These kinds of screen shots are really helpful when delivering a "how to" presentation, and so it's important to know the most efficient method to obtain exactly the image you need.

The 2010 and 2013 versions of PowerPoint have made adding a screenshot much simpler than previous versions.

To insert a screenshot:

1. Open a separate window for the image you want to incorporate into your PowerPoint file.

2. In the window you opened in Step 1, acquire or create the image you need for your presentation.

3. Modify or edit the image so that the screen looks *exactly* how you want the image to look in your presentation. If necessary, position the cursor exactly where you'd like it to appear for the screenshot.

4. Go back into PowerPoint and select *Insert -> Screenshot*, which is under the *Images* section. A cascade window will appear showing all of the windows you have open on your desktop (Figure 4.9).

Figure 4.9 Screenshot Cascade Window

5. Select the window displaying the image you just created. This image will then appear on your slide.

The *Insert-> Screenshot* feature (pictured above) will solve most of your screen capture needs, but sometimes you'll want a specific menu or screen that is only visible when your cursor is positioned on a certain option. Once you move the cursor away from that specific option, the menu disappears. For example, if you need to train employees to use a new software program, you will likely need specific screenshots of tools, menus, and options that are only visible for certain functions. You can proceed through your software to find the window or feature you need, but once you move out of the actual application (and back into PowerPoint to insert the screenshot), the cascade menu is no longer displayed. How can you take pictures of menus or windows that are only visible as long as your cursor doesn't move? You can use the *PrtScr* function key from your keyboard to capture images that require the cursor to be in a certain position.

To use the Print Screen function for image capture:

1. Open a separate window for the image you want to capture.

2. In the new window, acquire or create the image you need for your presentation.

3. Position the cursor as necessary to display the specific menu or window you need to capture.

4. Press the *PrtScr* button (location will depend on your specific keyboard) (Figure 4.10).

Figure 4.10 PrsScr

5. Go back into PowerPoint and click on the slide where you'd like the image to appear. Select *Control -> V* to paste the image onto the slide. The image will appear on your slide.

The *PrtScr* function will capture the entire window, but this might be more than you need, so you can *Crop* the image as necessary.

Save a Formatted Picture or Image

Once you acquire a picture and make your edits, you may want to save your modified image as a standalone file, to use it for another presentation, or just to keep a separate copy.

To save your image as a standalone file:

1. Right-click on the border of the image.

2. Select *Save as Picture*.

3. Assign a name and choose the desired location and file format.

Align Text Boxes or Objects

Often you may want more than one text box or more than one image on the same slide. Multiple objects will probably require some alignment for the slide to look "balanced." The *Align* feature in PowerPoint is useful to ensure you follow the design principle of Alignment. Not only can you align objects (pictures, text boxes, shapes) according their left or right margins, but this feature also is useful to help position objects in space and follow the design principle of Proximity.

Let's say you want to divide your text into two columns. You can use a pre-designed slide layout to make sure the two text boxes are aligned, or you may add them later and just want to manually align them yourself. Using your own judgment to determine whether they are properly aligned, or even centered, often doesn't work. The *Align* feature keeps you from having to guess or manually adjust the spacing yourself.

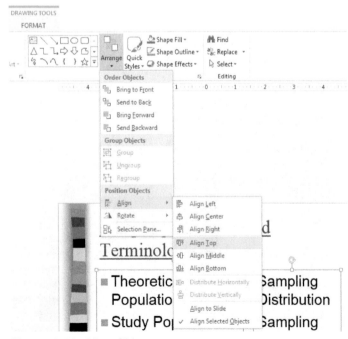

Figure 4.11 Align Objects

To align two or more objects:

1. Select all of the objects you wish to align (You will need to hold down the Shift key while selecting everything you'd like to include).

2. From the Home tab, select *Arrange -> Align -> Align Top*. Note that the Arrange option is within the category labeled *Drawing* under the *Home tab*.

The *Align* menu will also give you options to align your objects in many other ways as shown above. Learning to use the various options of the Align feature will help make sure your slide content is well-balanced and properly aligned.

Group Multiple Objects

Once you've aligned your objects, you might want to treat them as a group instead of individually. For example, you may add more objects or shapes, but you want the objects to move in unison with each other. Instead of having to individually realign them every time you need to move them, you can group them together so they are treated as one object. This can save you lots of time when trying to place multiple objects on your slide.

To group two or more objects:

1. Select all of the objects you wish to group (You will need to hold down the *Shift* key while selecting everything you'd like to include, or alternately you can draw one large box around all the objects you want to include and all objects will be selected. Click on any individual item to deselect it.)

2. From the *Home* tab, select *Arrange -> Group* (Figure 4.12).

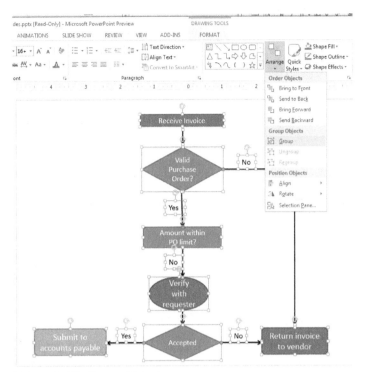

Figure 4.12 Group Objects

Use Smart Art

You can insert many different types of objects to create any kind of graphic you might need on a slide. For example, if you are trying to illustrate a process, you could insert or add each component of the process manually by inserting the objects individually and then connecting them with individually created lines or arrows. Although this isn't difficult, it is a bit time-consuming to create the objects, align them appropriately, and group them for later editing. If you need to make changes, then you must ungroup them, and adjust each individual object, which will require even more time. Alternatively, PowerPoint offers a collection of commonly used graphic layouts that are useful for displaying the components of any process on a slide. You can adjust the spacing and proximity of the components in the graphic layout, as needed to accomplish your visual goal.

First you must decide exactly what type of concept you are trying to convey. Ideally, you thought about a visual display for your idea in the Visualization stage of developing your speech content. If not, then you now need to think about the best way to illustrate your idea. Are you trying to communicate a list of items, a sequential process, or a repetitive cycle? Once you have determined your actual design, you can use the *SmartArt* feature in PowerPoint to help illustrate your idea.

To use SmartArt:

1. From the *Insert* tab, select *SmartArt*. This will bring up Figure 4.13.

From this screen, you can choose the graphic, which most closely represents your content.

The left pane lists the various types of graphics such as a list, a cycle, or a hierarchy of elements. You can click on one of the types of graphics, and then various

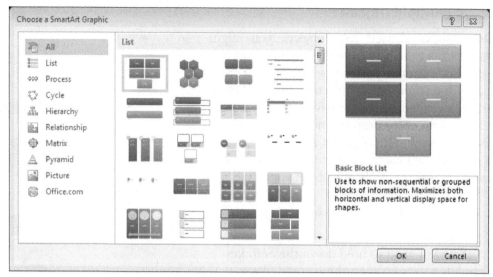

Figure 4.13 Smart Art Graphics

layouts for that type of graphic appear in the middle pane. Click on the layout that seems best, and it appears in the right pane, in color, and exactly as it will appear on the slide in your presentation. This visual display includes a description of how to enter text in each element in the graphic display.

2. Choose the layout you want to use and select *OK*. This will bring up the *SmartArt* tool bar, which allows you to modify the basic design to fit your needs. You can add objects or text, and change the colors and font of the *SmartArt* object.

3. Enter your text and you will see the graphic dynamically change to fit your content, as in Figure 4.14.

As with many other features of PowerPoint, be careful not to over use *SmartArt* when it really doesn't help convey your idea. Make sure your content is enhanced by *SmartArt*, not overwhelmed by it.

3. Enhancing Slides

Once you've created a basic slide layout, you'll likely want to enhance and polish your presentation content. Although there are many options available in PowerPoint to help enhance your slides, three of the most useful are these:

- Change the Background
- Insert a Hyperlink
- Add Media

Change the Background

When you first began creating your slides, you may have chosen a template or edited the *Slide Master* to ensure consistency among all your

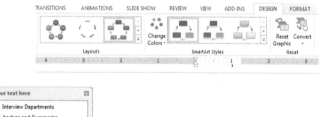

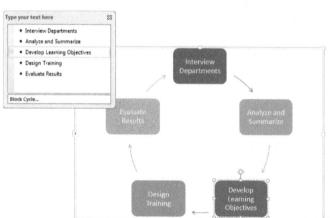

Figure 4.14 SmartArt Sample

slides. A template or *Slide Master* is a great time saving tool but, depending on your content, you may want to vary the background and use a picture or image to help emphasize or highlight an idea. Novice speakers might insert an image but it is too small, which limits the impact. You could try to enlarge the image (beware of pixilation), but depending on the scale, this may mean the image doesn't fit well on your slide.

A more effective option is to use your picture, but set it as the background for any text or data you need to display. This means your image would cover the entire slide.

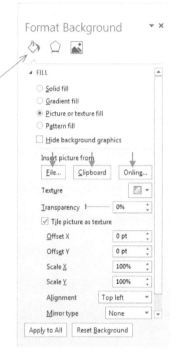

To set an image as the slide background:

1. Locate the image you want to use as the background (beware of copyright laws).

2. Under the Design tab, select *Format Background.*

3. Select *the Fill* icon to display the dialog box shown in Figure 4.15.

4. Select *Picture or texture fill*, and then chose *File . . .* to open a browser window. You can also use images stored on your *Clipboard* or search for photos *Online . . .*

5. Browse to locate the image you want to use, and click *Close* to choose that image. The selected image will become the full background for the slide you are working on. If you change your mind, simply select *Reset Background* to revert to your original layout before selecting *Close*.

Figure 4.15 Background Options

As with other available features, use this option sparingly. You don't want to overwhelm your audience with image after image, when it's the content, and your narration of it, that is most important. If you really want the image, but need to overlay text on top, use the *Transparency* feature to soften the image so the text will stand out better. However, be careful that your text and image don't visually compete with each other for your viewer's focus.

Insert a Hyperlink

One of the biggest criticisms of PowerPoint is that it forces you into a linear presentation format—moving sequentially from one slide to the next—and that doesn't always suit your content. Hyperlinks can help alleviate this linearity. ***Hyperlinks*** allow you to link or jump to another location, either within the software or outside the application, based on the location or address you specify. Hyperlinks are "linked" to text or an object on your slide, so that when you click on the object, the software "jumps" directly to the location you have specified. You can create links to:

▼ Hyperlinks
allow you to jump to another location, either within the software or outside the application, based on the location or address you specify.

- Slides within your presentation

- Existing files or web pages (like You Tube)

- Other documents

- E-mail addresses

Learning to use hyperlinks properly and smoothly can expand your content by allowing access to additional material outside of PPT, but still controlled from within the PowerPoint presentation.

Move to Another Slide within Your Slide Show:

1. On your slide, highlight the text or object you want to link to.

2. Select *Insert -> Hyperlink*.

3. Select *Place in This Document*. This will bring up a dialog box that displays a list of all the slides in your presentation (See Figure 4.16).

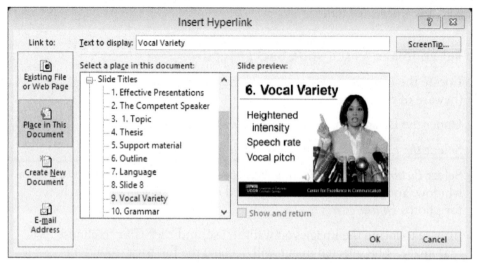

Figure 4.16 Insert Hyperlink

4. Select one of your existing slides from the box titled *Select a place in this document:* This will show a preview of that particular slide in the *Slide preview:* box.

5. Click *OK* to save your link.

Make sure to actually *link* your hyperlink to text or an image (*Simplicity*). Don't just display the hyperlink text.

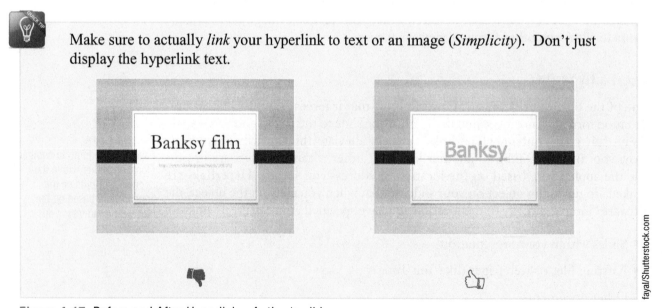

Figure 4.17 Before and After Hyperlink – Author's slides

Remember that if you create a hyperlink to another slide in your presentation, you also need to create a link to return to the slide you jumped from. Here's how you do that.

Create a Return Link:

1. Select the text or object for your return link.

2. From the *Insert* tab, select *Action* (See Figure 4.18.).

3. Select *Hyperlink to:* and choose the slide you'd like to return to.

4. Click *OK*.

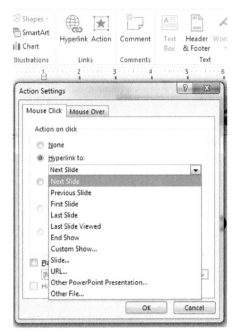

When you return to your original slide, you will notice that the selected text color has changed to a light blue. Depending on the color scheme of your slide show, you may want to change the high-light color of a hyperlink. Here's how you do that.

Change the Color of Hyperlinked Text:

1. From the *View tab*, select *Slide Master*.

2. In the *Background* section, Click *Colors -> Customize Colors*. This will bring up the dialog box shown in Figure 4.19.

3. Select *Hyperlink* and choose a highlight color that works with your specific color theme. *Followed Hyperlink* refers to the color of the text once you return to your original slide.

Figure 4.18 Return Link

4. Click *Save*.

In addition to linking from one slide to another within your presentation, you also may want to include content from outside the PowerPoint software program. You have many options available for using outside content to help communicate your message. These sources include, but are not limited to, websites, maps, other software and tools, and videos from YouTube. In an effort to keep the size of your presentation file small (by not embedding in it all the content you need for your presentation), you can use hyperlinks to "jump out" of the PowerPoint application and navigate directly to the Internet or other media sources. However, embedded hyperlinks are much more seamless than switching back and forth between windows on your computer, and, when used well, will appear far more professional. far more professional. Whether to embed content or not is addressed further in the next section.

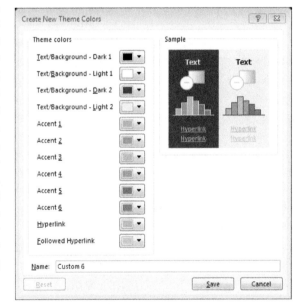

Figure 4.19 Hyperlink Colors

Add Media

Today's speakers must be prepared to incorporate video and/or audio components into their presentations. Plenty of high quality material is available to help you com-municate your message, but don't get carried away. Just because you can find plenty of video content, that doesn't mean you should use it all. As with any content decision, make sure you have the audience in mind as well as the purpose of your presentation.

Before you can add or insert video or audio, we need to clarify one issue. If you use a hyperlink to jump to a video, on another website for example, the video resides on <u>that other website</u>. To insert that video into your presentation, the video file must reside <u>on your computer</u>. This means you must have a digital copy (or original) of the audio or video file you intend to use in your presentation. You can use third-party software to obtain a digital copy from other sources, but as with images, similar copyright laws apply to video and audio.

Also, inserting video or audio files can substantially increase your file size and make presentations difficult to email or store. If you add video or audio, you may want to also compress your media to save space and improve performance (found under *File -> Info-> Compress Media*). Note: If you are using a Mac computer and depending on the PPT version that you are using, the *Compress Media* option may not be available. You will need to compress the video BEFORE inserting into the PPT file.

Insert a Video:

1. Click on the slide where you would like the video to appear.

2. Select *Insert -> Video*,

3. Choose your video source—*Online Video . . .*, or *Video on My PC . . .* For this example, we will use *Video on My PC. . .*

   If you select *Online Video. . .*, a browser will appear for you to search on line or embed a video code from a website (i.e., YouTube). Even if you "embed" a video, viewers will need an Internet connection to watch the video during your presentation. See the *PowerPoint Help* manual for specific embed code instructions.

4. Locate the file on your PC and double-click. The video will appear in a rectangle at the center of your slide. You can use the resize handles to make the box larger, but remember you risk distorting the image quality. Be sure to check the visual display on the screen you will use for your presentation.

   Once you have inserted your video, you can then edit it, much as you would as any image, using these tools from the *Format* tab.

Figure 4.20 Media Tools

To edit the content of the video and how it appears in your presentation, you will need another set of tools.

Edit a Video:

1. Select the video you wish to edit

2. Click the *Playback* tab on the menu at the top of your screen. This will bring up a different set of tools with which to edit and adjust your video.

   Using the *Playback options* menu shown in Figure 4.21, you can:

Figure 4.21 Video Playback Options

- Play the video to check for quality

- Add a Bookmark to indicate specific points in the video clip

- Trim the video

- Edit the fade in and fade out timing

- Adjust the volume

- Create a video loop

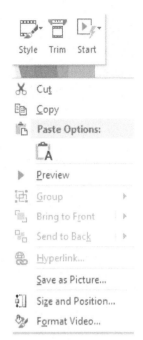

Figure 4.22 Video Formatting Options

Often, you will need only a small portion of a video in your presentation; showing too much of it may, in fact, become boring. The 2010 and 2013 versions of PowerPoint allow you to trim the front and back ends of a video to help isolate only the part you need. This can save your audience from having to watch content that isn't relevant to your message. Note: If you are using a Mac computer, and depending on the PPT version that you are using, the *Trim Video* option may not be available. You will need to trim the video BEFORE inserting into the PPT file.

Trim a Video:

1. Right-click on the video on your slide, which brings up the menu of formatting options shown in Figure 4.22.

2. Select *Trim*, which brings up Figure 4.23. This dialog box displays the controls for trimming the beginning and end of your video file.

3. Drag the green and red bars or use the arrow keys to trim the video, so it will start and end exactly where you'd like it to. You will see the start and end time counter change as you trim the video. Knowing exactly how long your video will take is important to determining your total speaking time.

4. Remember to select *OK* to save your changes to the video.

Figure 4.23 Trim Video

Trimming a video allows you to use only the portion of the video that you need. However, sometimes you might need several excerpts from one video file, but these segments are not consecutive. Instead of inserting the video multiple times (which really impacts file size), you can set bookmarks to indicate the point or points (in the video) to which you want to jump. Bookmarks are far more convenient than trying to remember the exact time point in the video and fast forwarding to that point.

Add a Bookmark:

1. Click on the video where you would like to add a bookmark (make sure you're not still in the *Trim Video* tool).

2. Select the play button to begin playing the video.

3. At the point where you wish to insert a bookmark, click the pause button in the time bar at the bottom of the video.

4. Select *Add Bookmark*. The bookmarks will appear as small dots at each point that you select.

Inserting audio is very similar to inserting video and many of the tools are almost the same. As with video, you must have a digital copy of the audio file you want to insert. Microsoft also provides many common audio sounds, but don't use any audio, unless it truly adds to your audience's understanding.

Insert Audio:

1. Click on the slide where you would like the Audio icon to appear.

2. Select *Insert -> Audio.* This brings up a browser window to search online, on your computer, or record an audio file.

    PowerPoint 2013 includes an option to record your own audio without additional software. However, we recommend a headset with microphone for better sound quality. You can add any type of sound or narration to your presentation. This is an excellent option for self-running presentations or lectures.

3. Click on the file you want to use, then click the *Insert* button. The icon representing your audio will appear in the center of your slide. You can resize this icon as required, or move it to a more appropriate location on your slide.

    Once you have added audio, you have multiple options to edit the audio for your specific purpose. For example you can trim the audio in the same way as trimming video.

    Using the *Audio Tools* menu shown below (Figure 4.24), you can:

Figure 4.24 Audio Playback Options

- Play the audio to check for sound
- Add a Bookmark to indicate specific points in the audio
- Trim the audio
- Edit the fade in and fade out timing
- Adjust the volume
- Create an audio loop
- Set the Audio to play in the Background

Thus far, we have discussed creating basic slides, inserting pictures and objects on slides, and enhancing the visual appeal of slides in general. We now turn our attention to using PowerPoint effectively to create tables and figures.

4. Building Tables and Figures

In many cases, your content will be better illustrated using a table or a chart. Tables are an excellent choice for data that is too cumbersome to be presented in a typical paragraph, especially data that includes numbers or dollar amounts.

The format for a table resembles a spreadsheet and has columns and rows. When planning your table, first think about the layout and the text to be displayed as headings for the columns and rows. That information helps you choose a table in PowerPoint to insert on your slide or slides.

Insert a Table:

1. Click on the slide where you would like the table to appear.

2. Select *Insert -> Table*. This brings up Figure 4.25 that you use to determine the number of rows and columns you will need for your data.

3. Click in the top left corner of this dropdown menu and drag your cursor to highlight the number of columns and rows you will need. As you scroll to select the dimensions of your table, the actual table will dynamically adjust to match your selection.

Note: Be sure to allow extra rows for column headings and sub-headings (if necessary).

4. When you have selected what you need, let go of the mouse and your table will be presented on the slide.

If you would like to make changes to your table, by adding or deleting rows or columns, or altering the layout, click on the border of this table, and the *Edit Table* toolbar will be visible (Figure 4.26).

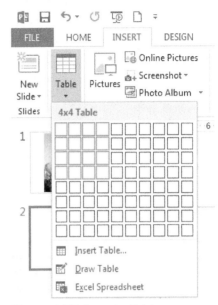

Figure 4.25 Insert a Table

Figure 4.26 Edit Table

Using this toolbar, you can change many of the color and shading options, line widths, and borders of your table. Here are two examples of this basic approach to creating tables.

Increase in Sales

Month	Revenue 2011	Revenue 2012	Percent Increase
January	$20,061.81	$28,075.98	39.9%
February	$24,844.46	$27,644.53	11.3%
March	$24,330.10	$41,593.20	70.9%

Figure 4.27 Sales Table

Healthiest States

State	BMI Score
Colorado	20.1
Utah	21.6
Connecticut	21.7
California	22.1
Rhode Island	22.1

Figure 4.28 Healthiest States Table

Tables are fairly simple, but are sometimes overused. Often the data represented in a table might be better illustrated using another type of graphic such as a bar chart, pie chart, or line graph, as described in Part III. To decide which type of table or figure to use, you must first determine exactly what you are trying to communicate with your data. For example, if you are comparing things, a bar graph would be a better choice than a pie chart. If you're trying to indicate a trend, then a line graph is probably your best option. Bar charts and line graphs are created in a similar manner, and have common elements.

▼ **Column**
Column charts represent data using bars that are positioned vertically.

It's important to note here that PowerPoint differentiates between column and bar charts. **Column** charts represent bars that are positioned vertically. A **Bar** chart displays data bars that are positioned horizontally. Think about the data you are trying to display and choose the one that you think is most appropriate for those data and for your audience.

Create a Bar Chart or Line Graph:

1. Click on the slide where you would like the chart or graph to appear.

2. Select *Insert -> Chart*. This brings up a menu for you to select among several different possible layouts (Figure 4.29). For a vertical bar chart, select *Column*. For a *Line graph*, select *Line*.

Figure 4.29 Insert Chart

	A	B	C	D
1		COS	GSO	SAN
2	2009	50,000	153,000	35,000
3	2010	78,000	88,000	75,000
4	2011	201,000	230,000	150,000
5	2012	137,000	161,000	135,000

Figure 4.30 Chart Data

3. Select the style you want and click *OK*.
A window will open that resembles a spreadsheet with a template of rows and columns for you to enter your data.

4. Enter your data into the spreadsheet, and it will immediately appear on a chart or graph on your slide. The row labels will become the horizontal axis data, and the column headings will be used in the legend.

For example, the table in Figure 4.30 shows the data used to generate the XYZ Company's line graph that follows in Figure 4.31.

The elements common to both a bar chart and line graph are shown in Figure 4.31 in the blue boxes. It is important you become familiar with editing and manipulating these elements to make sure you don't end up with *Chartjunk*. **Chartjunk** refers to any visual element on a chart or graph that isn't necessary to the audience's understanding of the data. In keeping with the *Simplicity* principle, from the *SCRAP* method in Part III, you should eliminate all "chartjunk." Remember our recommendation to "*SCRAP* the crap!" To do this, you will need to decide what must be on the graph for easy comprehension, and what you need to say so the audience understands the message inherent in the data.

▼ **Chartjunk**
refers to any visual element on a chart or graph that isn't necessary to the audience's understanding of the data.

Here are some suggestions to help you reduce "chartjunk" on your slides:

1. *Data Labels* – All data labels are not shown in the XYZ Company's line graph, because it would be too much information, especially for a slide. Only a few labels are shown to indicate what they look like.

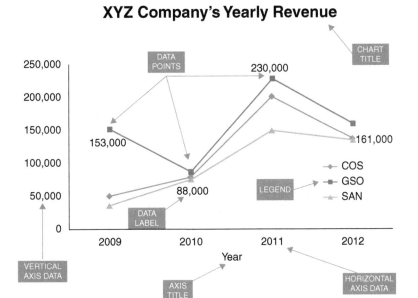

Figure 4.31 Line Graph

2. *Decimal Places* – If your original data includes decimal places, you may want to round the numbers to the nearest whole number.

3. *Legend* – The legend is often unnecessary because either the displayed units are obvious, or because you can easily explain what each line represents.

And another important note—to change the data in your chart or graph, make changes in the spreadsheet, not the chart or graph.

Edit a Bar Chart or Line Graph:

1. Select the graph representing the data you would like to edit.

2. From the *Design* tab, select *Edit Data*. This will bring up your spreadsheet in which you can edit the data, just as you would in *Excel*.

Create a Pie Chart:

Pie charts are a good visual choice when you are trying to show how individual components contribute to a whole unit, or when your percentages will better display your data. As with bar charts and line graphs, many of the elements can be manipulated for a clearer display.

1. Click on the slide where you would like the pie chart to appear.

2. Select *Insert -> Chart*. This brings up a menu on which you can select the layout. You can choose an exploded layout initially ("slices" are separated and not touching each other) or change to this format later.

3. Select *Pie*. A spreadsheet window will open for you to enter data. Depending on your data type, you may want to enter your data with decimals.

4. Click on your slide and a basic pie chart and *Legend* will appear. The *Legend* will show the row headings you entered into the spreadsheet.

From here you need to edit your pie chart to display your data more clearly to your audience. A pie chart includes some of the elements of a bar chart and line graph, but obviously some don't apply.

The first place to begin your edit is to format the *Data Labels*. Initially, *Data Labels* do not appear on the pie slices, but you may want them there for clarification (but, beware of "chartjunk").

Figure 4.33 Data Label Options

Add Data Labels:

1. Click on your pie chart.

2. Click the *Chart Elements* icon.

3. Select *Data Labels* to expand the menu.

4. Scroll down and select *More Options . . .* Alternately, you can right-click directly on the "pie" to bring up a menu and select *Format Data Labels.*

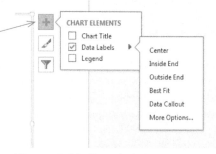

Figure 4.32 Data Labels

Either method will bring up the window shown in Figure 4.33.

From here, you can choose the text and data you would like to appear on the actual pie slices and the positions for those labels. In the following pie chart of "Expenses" (Figure 4.34), the data labels and positions are based on the selections in the window above.

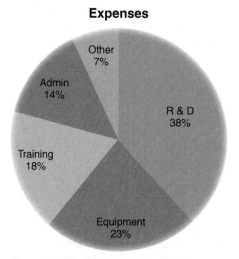

Figure 4.34 Expenses Pie Chart

Series Name   Refers to the title of the pie chart (i.e. "Expenses"). By default, the *Series Name* appears directly above the image, but the default placement usually does not adhere to basic design principles of text size, balance, or proximity. For the pie chart in Figure 4.34, we did not select this option. Instead we placed the title, "Expenses," outside the pie, so we could edit and position it for the best alignment.

Category Name   Refers to the name of the individual pie slices (i.e. "R & D, Equipment, Training, and Admin").

Value   Refers to the number displayed on the pie slices (in the Figure 4.34 pie chart, the numbers are formatted as percentages)

Leader Lines   Refer to lines, which connect the *Category Name* to the specific pie segment. *Leader Lines* only appear when the *Category Name* will not fit in the pie segment (i.e. "Other").

PowerPoint 2013 allows you to place the actual data, like the percentages and their labels, in separate positions. If you move any label outside of the pie, a leader line will be added automatically. You can manually add any other label you feel will be necessary. Once you have added the labels you need, you can edit any individual text or data unit. For example, you may want to emphasize the "largest slice" by increasing the text size of that specific data label, while keeping the other labels the same, smaller text size.

In the "Expenses" pie chart, the slices "touch" each other. But sometimes for **emphasis**, you may want to separate your segments, which results in "exploding" the pie. If you didn't initially explode, here is how you can add this feature after you create the pie chart.

Explode pie slices:

1. Right-click on your pie chart, which brings up a menu.

2. From this menu, select, *Format Data Series . . .* and the window in Figure 4.35 will appear.

3. Select the single "slice" you'd like to separate from the rest of the pie chart.

4. Under *Point Explosion*, drag the indicator to the desired level of separation of the pieces that you prefer. You will see your "piece" move as you drag the indicator.

5. Click on your slide to save your changes.

In Figure 4.36, the pie slices will be separated from one another to the degree you've specified. In the exploding pie the largest slice, labeled *Research*, is separated from the rest of the pie. The legend has also been positioned across the bottom (instead of the default right side) to better balance the images on the slide.

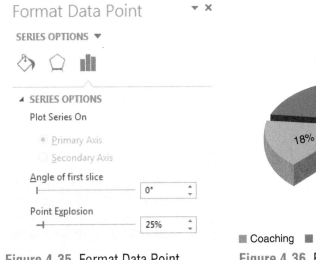

Figure 4.35 Format Data Point

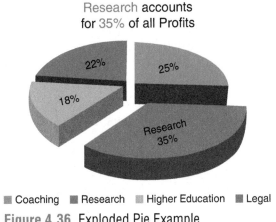

Figure 4.36 Exploded Pie Example

Make sure the colors of your pie don't produce the 'the fruit salad' effect, but complement the overall presentation theme (*Repetition*). Use a larger font size and color to highlight the most important information and make it easier to read (*Contrast*).

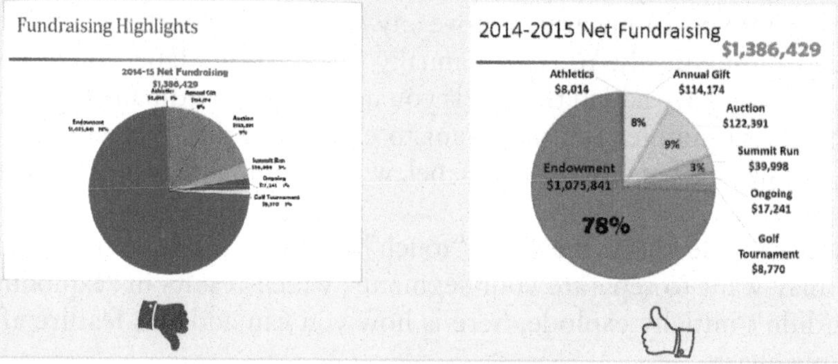

Figure 4.37 Before and After Pie chart – Author's slides

We now consider how you can use animation to create interest and excitement to your PowerPoint slides.

5. Adding Animation

Thinking visually and including images in your presentations is definitely a good beginning for becoming a more effective speaker. But sometimes, the static presentation of information is not enough to adequately convey your ideas. Animation often is a more effective way to present some types of information and concepts. For example, if you need to describe a process or sequence of events, adding animation to illustrate progression among steps will have a greater impact than displaying the steps in the process all at once. Animation can be a powerful tool for speakers who want to:

- **Prevent the audience from "reading ahead" and not listening to you** You can use animation to have your bullets appear one at a time, so the audience doesn't read ahead of you. This is probably the most underutilized PPT feature.

- **Illustrate complex concepts** You can manipulate the appearance of, and movement of, objects to "look inside" a diagram.

- **Enhance the description of a sequence of events** You can visually depict a process by animating the steps thereby "simulating" a real-time occurrence.

- **Create movement on the screen to emphasize specific information** You can use highlighting and emphasis to help the audience focus on a specific point or object. Using an animated arrow to point to a specific area on the slide is an excellent way to focus the audience's attention (See Figure 4.38).

However, before we go any further, a quick caution regarding animation is necessary. Many speakers, novices and seasoned veterans, use flashy functions in PowerPoint, even when these functions add little to understanding the presentation. In some cases, too much animation may even detract from your message because the audience pays more attention to the moving objects on the screen than to you. As with any other tool, the overriding question is, "Will it enhance my audience's understanding of my topic?" Flashing objects and dazzling transitions and exit effects likely won't do much for audience comprehension, so "animate" wisely.

Move the components of a graph, such as the legend or numbers, to suit your presentation needs (*Proximity*). Use arrows or color, especially on a busy data slide, to draw attention to specific content (*Contrast*). Animating the arrows to appear only when you are ready, gives you greater control and flexibility.

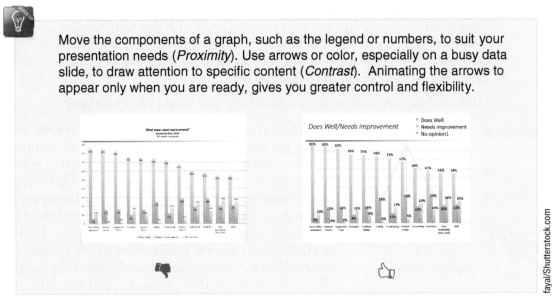

Figure 4.38 Before and After Animation

Animate Bullet Points:

Although we spent a good bit of time in Parts II and III trying to get you to think about images that could replace your text, there will likely always be a slide or two that contains bullet points. This doesn't mean your slide is bad. Bullet point slides can be very useful for an overview of your speech or main points, particularly when your presentation is instructional or a training that is information-intensive. You can use animation to make even a bullet point slide more visually appealing and interesting and thus keep the audience from "reading ahead. Here's how.

1. Create your bullet points using a basic text box. Remember to use as few words as possible, make the lines parallel, and use as large a font size for text as feasible.

2. Select the specific text you would like to animate (likely one bullet at a time).

3. From the *Animation* tab, select *Add Animation* right above "Advanced Animation." The dialog box shown in Figure 4.39 will appear.

This dialog box provides a list of options for you to determine how your text will initially appear on the slide (*Entrance effects*), disappear from the slide (*Exit effects*), or to add emphasis (*Emphasis*) to some portion. Additional options are listed at the bottom of the dialog box, but in most cases, the displayed options are all you will need.

4. Choose the effect you'd like to see for your text. For our purposes, we like to keep it simple and use *Appear*. Although PowerPoint offers many options, most of them are too flashy and will likely detract from your message.

Figure 4.39 Animation Effects

Once you've chosen an effect, a small number will appear to the left of your text to indicate an animation effect is associated with this text. Successive numbers will be generated to indicate multiple animations associated with this text. For example, if you add both an *Entrance effect* and an *Exit effect*, you will see two numbers to the left of the text.

5. Repeat these steps for each segment of text you would like to animate.

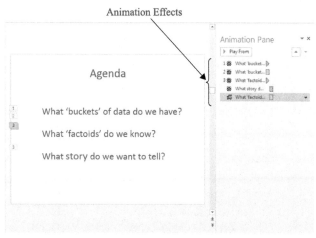

Figure 4.40 Animation Pane

When creating your slides, you may decide to rearrange the order in which the bullet points appear or disappear. The *Animation Pane* dialog box, accessed in "Advanced Animation," easily facilitates such rearrangement. The *Animation Pane* displays all animation effects, and these effects will occur in the sequence shown in this pane. The Animation Pane in Figure 4.40 shows five animation effects for three bulleted lines of text on the slide. Notice that three effects are shown with a green star, and two effects with a red star. Green stars indicate an *Entrance effect* and red stars depict an *Exit effect*. This will help you determine exactly which animation effect you are editing.

If you look carefully in the *Animation Pane*, you will see that the first line of text is animated to appear (#1) and disappear (#2) before the second bullet point ever shows on the slide. This is probably not what you intended, and therefore, you need to reorder these effects so that all three bullet points appear before any bullet points disappear. We'll cover control and timing of these effects shortly.

Reorder Bullet Points:

1. In the *Animation Pane*, click on the bullet you'd like to move in the sequence.

2. Click on the reorder arrows at the top of the *Animation Pane* to move the text up or down as necessary.

3. You can use the *Play* button at the top of the *Animation Pane* to see your changes take effect. This may take several "trial and error" attempts to animate the bullets exactly as you want them to appear and disappear during your presentation.

Adjust Object Effects

There are many other ways you can enhance your slides by using animation. Sometimes you want an effect to happen when you click the mouse, other times you may want it to occur when something else happens on the screen, such as the end of a video. In conjunction with your animation, you may choose to adjust the timing of the effect, so it coincides with your narration.

1. In the *Animation Pane*, click on the object for which you'd like to modify the timing.

2. Click on the down arrow directly to the right of this object. This will bring up the menu (Figure 4.41).

3. Select the effect you would like to modify.

This menu allows you to adjust timing as well as other useful options.

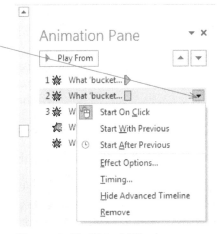

Start On Click –   Signals animation event to happen when mouse (or pointer) is clicked

Start With Previous –   Will begin animation at the same time as the previous effect takes place

Start After Previous –   Will begin animation immediately after the previous effect has completed (can be changed with timing options)

Effect Options . . . –   Allows you to specify the direction (when applicable) of the object's movement; also includes more options for timing and sequencing

Figure 4.41 Object Effects

Timing . . . –   Allows you to control the time to begin animations as well as delays between effects. It is *usually* preferable for you to control when text or objects appear, rather than to set the occurrence at a certain amount of time. When you actually present the speech, the set times may not work when and as you need.

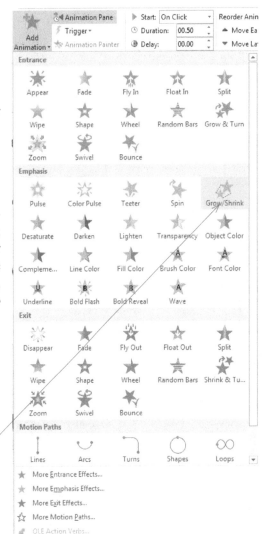

Hide Advanced Timeline –   A toggle to *Show* or *Hide* the timing bar at the bottom of the *Animation Pane*

Remove –   Deletes any animation (or multiple animations) from the animation sequence

In the slide in Figure 4.40, we showed you how to add animation to the three bullet points and then reorder them if necessary, but this is still a bit boring. After thinking further about your information, you may decide the real focus of this slide is the final bullet point—"What story do we want to tell?" Therefore, to emphasize this question more than the first two, you need to adjust the animation to include an emphasis effect.

Add Emphasis Effect

1. Animate the three bullets to appear, one at a time (as described earlier).

2. Select the text for the third bullet and choose an *Emphasis* effect from the *Add Animation* pane. In this case, let's use *Grow/Shrink.*

3. For maximum impact, add an *Exit* effect to the first two bullets, as the third bullet appears. (Have them disappear from the screen).

PowerPoint will automatically place these two new *Exit* effects at the bottom of your animation sequence, so you may need to

Figure 4.42 Emphasis Effect

reorder them. In keeping with the emphasis on the third question, you may want to reorder your effects to place the *Exit* effect before the appearance of the third bullet.

4. Adjust the timing of the *Grow/Shrink* effect, so it occurs a little more slowly. In the *Animation Pane*, select the arrow next to the *Grow/Shrink* effect. This will bring up a drop down menu with more options, as listed below.

5. Select *Timing. . .* and the dialog box in Figure 4.43 will appear.

Use the dialog box shown in Figure 4.43 to control these effects:

■ Onset of the effect (*Start: With Mouse Click, With Previous,* etc.)

■ Timing of the effect (*Delay:*)

■ Speed of the effect (*Duration:*). The default is *0.5 seconds (Very Fast).*

■ Number of iterations of the effect (*Repeat:*)

If you completed all the steps outlined above, to have the first two bullets appear, then disappear, and the third bullet to appear, and grow larger, your *Animation Pane* would look like the one immediately to the right in Figure 4.44. Notice the yellow rectangle to the right of the *Emphasis* effect, which indicates that the timing of the effect is adjusted to be slower than the default.

Figure 4.43 Animation Timing

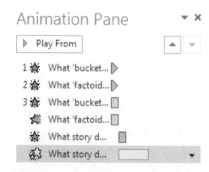

Figure 4.44 Final Animation Pane

To make it simpler, and reduce clicking, most of the functions we just described are also easily available from the top of the *Animation* Toolbar (Figure 4.45).

Another option, accessed from either the *Timing* dialog box or the *Animation* Toolbar, is *Trigger* (Figure 4.46).

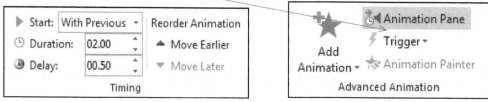

Figure 4.45 Simplified Timing

Figure 4.46 Trigger

The default start for any animation effect is mouse click, but *Trigger* allows you to specify these two other start options:

- *On Click of* specific text displayed on the slide
- *On Bookmark* at a certain point in a video that you want to trigger the animation

Animate a Chart, Graph or *SmartArt* Object

Animation effects are useful for objects other than text including charts, graphs, and even *SmartArt* objects. Instead of showing the whole chart at once, and possibly overwhelming your audience, you can build the chart slowly, adding information as you narrate.

Adding animation to a column chart, line graph, or *SmartArt* is similar to animating text, but with a couple more steps.

1. Select the object you'd like to animate. Make sure the rectangular border surrounding the object is visible.

2. Select *Add Animation* from the *Animation* tab on the toolbar.

3. Select *Wipe* as your *Entrance effect*. You could choose any of the other options, but *Wipe* seems to fit the purpose of animating the bars in a bar chart.

By default, PowerPoint treats the entire chart as a single object, therefore, to animate parts of this object (individual shapes, bars, or lines), you need to make the *Animation Pane* visible.

4. Select *Animation Pane* from the toolbar.

5. In the *Animation Pane*, right-click on the down arrow to the right of the chart. This will bring up a drop-down menu.

6. Select *Effect Options* . . . This will bring up the dialog box shown in Figure 4.47.

We used this dialog box earlier when adjusting the *Timing* options for the *Emphasis* effect, but now we need to edit the *Chart Animation*.

7. Select the *Chart Animation* tab at the top. This will access a drop down menu for you to choose exactly what objects (like the bars perhaps), within the object, you would like to animate. You can animate the chart:

Figure 4.47 Chart Animation

- **As One Object:** Animated all at once

- **By Series:** All series animated at once

- **By Category:** All categories animated at once

- **By Element in Series:** All individual series elements animated sequentially

- **By Element in Category:** All individual category elements animated sequentially

In the bar graph shown in Figure 4.48, the bars represent three categories, so we've selected *By Category*. Depending on your data and graphic format, you can use these options to create very specific animations to suit your purpose.

FYI at the time of printing: No options are available to animate data labels, axes titles, or legends.

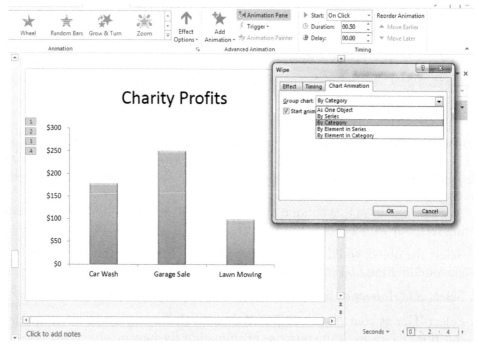

Figure 4.48 Animation by Category

By now, you know how to use PowerPoint to do five things: create basic slides, insert pictures and objects, enhance your slides, build tables and figures, and add animation. Using these functions you are now able to create a dynamic presentation. The last thing to learn about PowerPoint is how to generate and present the slide show most effectively.

6. Generating Your Slide Show

You've probably already used PowerPoint for presentations, so you're familiar with the *Slide Show* tab including how to begin your presentation (*From Beginning*) or start somewhere in the middle (*From Current Slide*). However, we would like to show you several additional features to help customize your delivery and polish your presentation.

Add Transitions

Once you have created all of the slides for your presentation, the next logical step is to determine how you will move from slide to slide within the presentation. PowerPoint offers many variations to transition between slides, but you don't need to use them all! Novice speakers sometimes get carried away with the flashy effects and use transitions to distraction.

Choose the transition that best suits your content and audience (Figure 4.49). If you are comparing your product to another company's product, then the *Push* or *Switch* transition might work well. If you are trying to build interest and suspense, then *Reveal* may be a good choice. Remember that any slide effect should not overshadow you as the speaker, so use transitions conservatively.

Create a Custom Slide Show

Most speakers create a new and unique slideshow for each new setting, even if the new presentation covers the same topic as the original presentation. Certainly

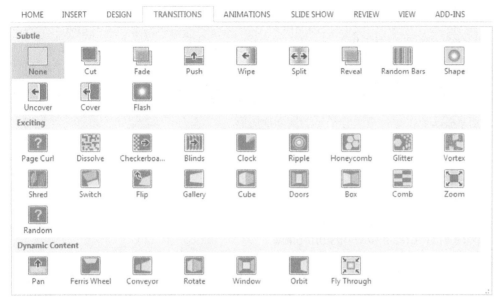

Figure 4.49 Transitions

creating a new slideshow for a new and different audience reinforces the idea of keeping the audience's needs foremost in mind, but it is time-consuming and somewhat inefficient. Most likely you would copy and paste slides from an older presentation into the new one, then add what you need for the particular situation. This is not necessarily a bad process, but there is a better way; especially if you have material that needs to be updated or changed frequently.

A more efficient method to create a slide show that covers the same topic, but for a different audience, is to create one slideshow and then customize it to show only those slides you need for the particular audience. The feature, *Custom Slide Show*, allows you to have a "master" slide show with subsets of slides segregated into smaller shows customized for a particular purpose and audience. Here are the steps involved.

1. Open the presentation you would like to customize.

2. Select the *Slide Show* tab from the toolbar.

3. Select *Custom Slide Show*, which will bring up the dialog box shown in Figure 4.50. In Figure 4.50, two custom shows have already been created—one for clients, and one for Investors.

   From the dialog box in Figure 4.50, you can edit, remove, or copy existing *Custom Shows*, or create a new one.

Figure 4.50 Custom Slide Show

4. To create a new *Custom Show*, select *New . . .* The dialog box in Figure 4.51 will appear.

5. Assign a *Slide show name*: and select the slides you would like to include in this custom show.

6. Click *Add* to place the selected slides into this Custom Show.

7. Click *OK* to save your custom show. Be sure you name it in a way that is easily identifiable by you in the future.

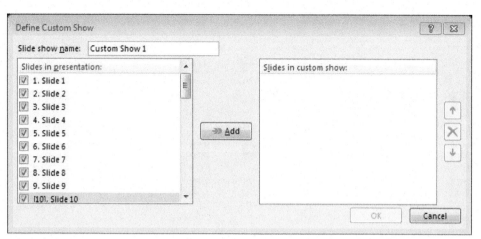

Figure 4.51 Create New Custom Show

Display a Custom Show

1. Open your PowerPoint file.

2. Select the *Slide Show* tab.

3. Select *Custom Slide Show*.

4. Select the *Custom Show* you would like to use.

   The show will run just like any other PowerPoint presentation.

Record Slide Timing

Giving a presentation normally requires you to stay within a finite time frame. Using *Record Slide Timing* is important to ensure you stay within the allotted time, yet don't miss any main points. Estimating the time you need to cover a topic is sometimes difficult for beginning speakers, but PowerPoint includes a feature to help practice the timing of your presentation *(Record Slide Timing)*. The more you practice your actual delivery, the more effective your presentation will be.

1. Select the *Slide Show* tab.

2. Select *Rehearse Timings*. This will bring up the *Rehearsal* toolbar, which displays the *Slide Time* box (Figure 4.52).

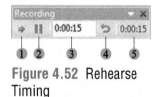

Figure 4.52 Rehearse Timing

This *Rehearsal* toolbar appears in the top left corner of your screen and your recording begins **immediately**.

1. *Next*, advance to the next slide.

2. *Pause*, temporarily stop recording.

3. *Slide Time*, set an exact length of time for the slide to appear.

4. *Repeat*, and restart recording for the current slide.

5. *Total*, the presentation time.

   You also can use *Record Slide Timings* to create a self-running presentation.

Create a Self-Running Presentations

The majority of presentations, using slides, are presented to a live audience, with a speaker narrating the slides. However, as technology continues to develop, other options for delivering presentations continue to grow. You may send your

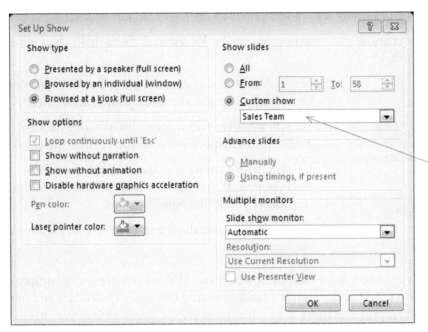

Figure 4.53 Set up Show

presentation to others for them to view on their own (*browsed by an individual*), or create a presentation that runs continuously in a booth at a conference. For either of these situations, you will need a self-running presentation. A ***self-running presentation*** runs automatically and doesn't require a speaker

▼ Self-running presentations are presentations that don't require a speaker.

1. Open your presentation and select the *Slide Show* tab.

2. Click *Set Up Slide Show*. This brings up the dialog box above in Figure 4.53.

3. Under *Show type*, choose the purpose of your self-running presentation.

The dialog box shown in Figure 4.53 indicates that the *Custom show* (Sales Team) will be browsed at a kiosk, and the slides advance based on pre-recorded time settings. You also have options to turn off any narration and animation, as the situation calls for.

Use the *Record Slide Timing* feature to set the slide timing options and/or action buttons, so viewers can progress through your presentation. Otherwise, your self-running presentation will not advance beyond the first slide.

Add Narration

If you are creating a self-running presentation that won't include a speaker, you may need to add narration. You can use the built-in microphone on your computer, but for better audio quality, you should invest in a headset with a microphone. This equipment is inexpensive and provides a more professional sound. Before you begin recording, make sure to test the microphone to be sure it is working properly. Here's how you add narration.

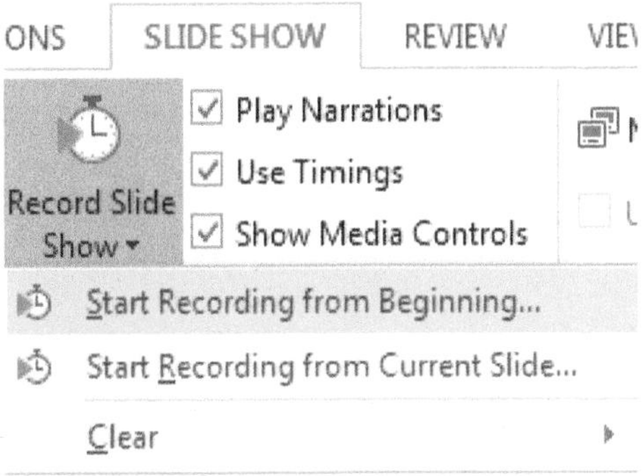

1. Open your PowerPoint file.

2. Select the *Slide Show* tab.

3. Select *Record Slide Show*.

4. Choose either *Start Recording from Beginning* . . . or from the current slide.

Figure 4.54 Record Slide Show

Clear provides options to delete previous timings and narrations.

Once you choose your starting point, the *Record Slide Show* dialog box appears (Figure 4.55).

Figure 4.55 Record Settings

5. Select *Narrations and laser pointer.* Turning this option on will also capture any laser pointer movement.

6. Decide whether you want slides to move forward automatically (specified with *Record Slide Timings*)

7. Click *Start Recording* and speak clearly into the microphone. If you need to stop in between slides, click on "Pause" and "Resume" buttons.

8. Right-click on the slide, and then select *End Show* to end the recording

This ends our discussion of PowerPoint. We did not present a comprehensive explanation of ALL the features available using this tool. The online and hard copy user manual provides more detail than most public speakers may ever need. On the other hand, we did try to highlight the critical functions available in PowerPoint that we think are:

■ Often misused

■ Often misunderstood

■ And, applicable and useful for most public speakers in most public speaking situations

As with any presentational tool, using PowerPoint effectively to achieve your public speaking goal is what really matters. By now, you probably realize that opening PowerPoint, finding a template you like, and filling in the blanks is not enough. Based on this new awareness, we now turn our attention to a brief description of another popular presentation software program—Prezi.

EXERCISES TO IMPROVE YOUR POWERPOINT SLIDES

1. Figure 4.56 shows two slides. Slide #1 you may remember from Part III. Using the information in Slide #1 (use your own logo from the Internet), and the appropriate PowerPoint tools, create Slide #2. You will need to change text color, align objects, alter spacing between text boxes, change slide background, and add design elements.

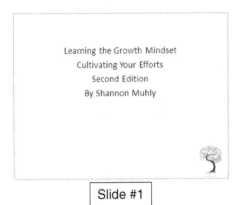

Figure 4.56 Before and After Title Slide

2. Search the Internet to determine the adoption process for your local Humane Society or pet shelter. Using the *SmartArt* feature, build an illustration to display the sequence of steps. Animate the *SmartArt* illustration to display each step at step at a time.

3. The slide below shows bullet points indicating an historical series of events.

> ### Important Dates
>
> - 597 - Capture of Jerusalem
> - 536 - Persia Captures Babylon
> - 535-513 - Temple re-building started
> - 464 - Artaxeres allows re-building to start
> - 457 - Artaxerxes allows self-government
> - 454 - Samaria report Jews and destroys walls and gates
> - 444 - Nehemiah visited in Susa

Figure 4.57 Bullet Point Slide

You realize this is a bit bland, so you want to add some "movement" to the slide. Your first instinct might be to:

a. Animate the bullet points to appear one at time, when you click the mouse.

 Although you now have "movement, the slide is still very "text heavy" and still BORING. If you try to apply **Visualization** to this content, you realize the text represents a timeline.

b. Convert these bullet points, into a timeline, that displays the events more pictorially.

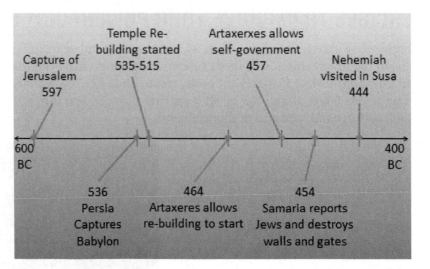

c. Now you can sequence the events to appear only when you are ready, so your listeners won't read ahead of you and potentially miss important information.

d. Animate the events to appear one at a time, when you click the mouse. Your *Animation Pane* might look something like this.

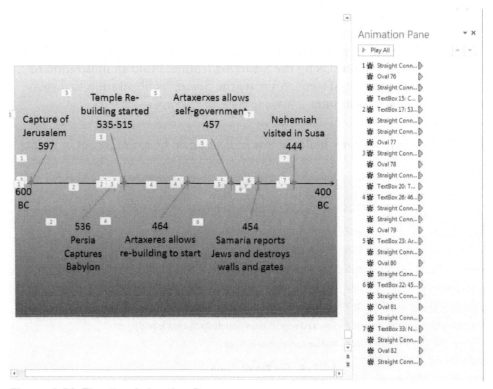

Figure 4.58 Timeline Animation Pane

4. Assume you are giving a sales presentation for your company. You might initially create a slide that looks like this one.

Sales	
2011	**2012**
January - 20,061.82	January - 28,075.98
February - 24,844.46	February - 27,644.53
March - 24,330.10	March - 41,593.20

Figure 4.59 Sales Data

a. You realize this display is boring, and you need to create a table to better present the data. Using the above figures, create a table similar to the one below. Experiment with changing the fill colors and column widths. Make sure your decimal points are aligned.

Increase in Sales

Month	Revenue 2011	Revenue 2012
January	$20,061.81	$28,075.98
February	$24,844.46	$27,644.53
March	$24,330.10	$41,593.20

Figure 4.60 Table of Sales Data

Although the table is nice and neat, it's still dull and not very visual. Is there an image that would better illustrate this information?

b. Since the information includes numbers, and the intent is a comparison of revenue in different time periods, a bar chart seems like an obvious choice. Using the table of data above, create a bar chart similar to the one below. Experiment with the *Data Labels* and *Axis Titles*.

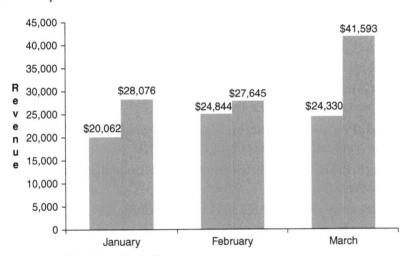

Figure 4.61 Sales Data Chart

c. To align the appearance of the bars with your narration, animate the bars so the 2011 sales figures (blue bars) appear, one at a time, followed by the 2012 sales figures (red bars), also one at a time.

5. If you completed Exercise #2 and created a slide to illustrate the adoption process for your local Humane Society or pet shelter, now add narration. You will need to use many of the *Slide show* and *Timing* features.

BUILDING PRESENTATIONS WITH PREZI

Prezi is a newer software program (launched in 2009) available to presenters for creating visuals to supplement presentations. Adam Somlai-Fischer, Prezi's co-creator, is an internationally renowned architect and visual artist who wanted to offer a different presentation tool to bring together both linear and non-linear thinking and provide a big picture perspective of how topics and ideas are related to one another.

▼ **Cloud-based applications** are software accessed using a web browser, but the actual software, data, and files are stored at a remote location.

Prezi is a cloud-based application that resides on the Internet as do the files you create. Users access *cloud-based applications* through a web browser, but the actual software, data, and files are stored at a remote location. Because Prezi is cloud-based, it is easier to collaborate with others when creating or sharing presentations. A maximum of ten people can be involved in creating and editing a Prezi presentation, which allows people, at different locations, to work together.

Since Prezi is an innovative software product, and still evolving and changing on a regular basis, we'll start at the very beginning and describe exactly how to use this somewhat new presentation tool. As Prezi developers continue to add features to the software, the windows and menus may change slightly, but the basic functionality remains the same.

1. Getting Started with Prezi

Open an Account

1. Navigate to the Prezi website: www.prezi.com.

2. Choose the specific licensing agreement that fits your needs:

   Public—core features, online creation only, all files are public, limited file storage, no annual fee

   Enjoy (EduEnjoy*)—core features, online creation only, larger file storage, more customization, annual fee

   Pro (EduPro*)—core features, even more storage capacity, customization, desktop version (for offline editing), annual fee

   Teams (EduTeams*)—core features, centralized billing, simple license management, training

   *Available to students and teachers with educational email addresses

3. Create an account (with login and password).

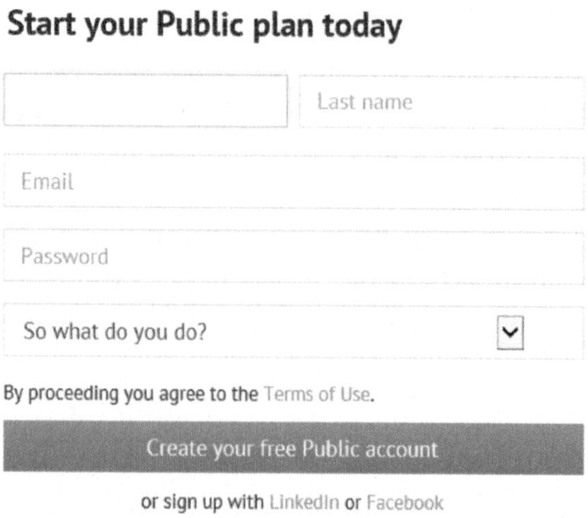

Start your Public plan today

	Last name

Email

Password

So what do you do? ∨

By proceeding you agree to the Terms of Use.

Create your free Public account

or sign up with LinkedIn or Facebook

Figure 4.62 Prezi Login Screen

Create a New Prezi

1. Once you are logged in, you will see your saved prezis.

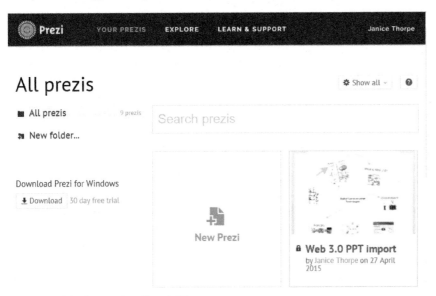

Figure 4.63 Accessing Prezi Files

After you create your first Prezi, all of your presentations will be displayed under *YOUR PREZIS*. The *LEARN & SUPPORT* link provides access to tutorials to help you use all of the features of the software. The *EXPLORE* link offers hundreds of examples (organized by content categories) of *Prezi*s available to you as a template for your own presentations. Viewing a few of these Prezis may help stimulate your thinking about what you want your presentation to look like.

2. Click on the *+ New prezi* box.

New Prezi

3. From the window that appears, choose a template that best represents the organization of your content. Then click *Use template*.

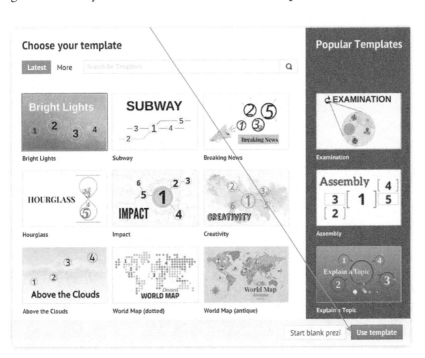

Figure 4.64 Prezi Templates

4. Name your file and describe its content. Then click *Create new prezi.*

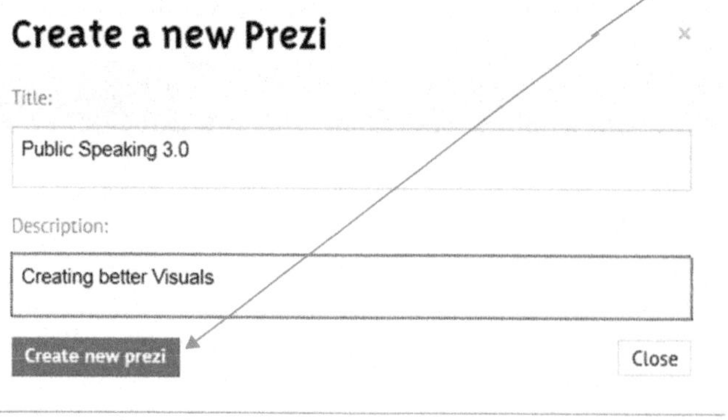

Create a new Prezi

Title:

Public Speaking 3.0

Description:

Creating better Visuals

Create new prezi   Close

Figure 4.65 Create New Prezi

This will bring up the selected canvas layout in which you can simply add your content to the pre-designed spaces. You can also choose a blank template if you would like to add the objects one at a time. If you are new to Prezi, using the pre-designed templates (canvas layouts) is an easy way to get started. Remember that the same design principles described in Part III of this book, apply to Prezi as well.

Once you've chosen a template, you will see the Prezi workspace. A few of the areas are labeled below, and we will introduce some of the tools as we go through the steps to create a Prezi.

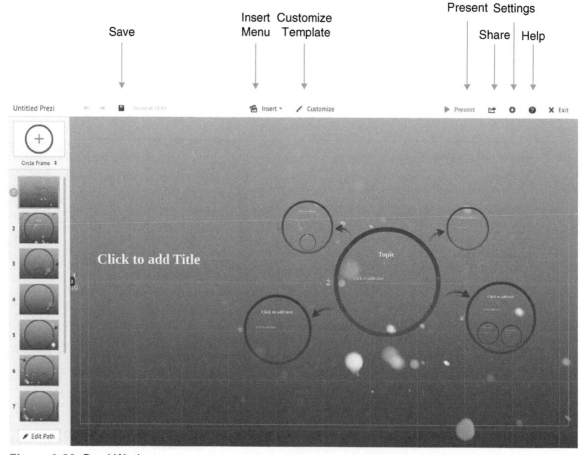

Figure 4.66 Prezi Workspace

Before we present the different tools and functions available, it's important that you understand how to move around in Prezi when creating your presentation. When you first open a new Prezi, you are automatically in *Edit* mode as opposed to *Present* mode (more on *Present* mode at the end of this discussion). The grid in the background is one indicator that you are in *Edit* mode. A second way to recognize which mode you're in is to move your cursor to the far right of the screen. You are in *Edit* mode if the *Home* and *Zoom* buttons fade into view. Becoming comfortable with moving around the canvas is the first task. **Canvas** is what Prezi calls the workspace you use for building your presentation.

▼ Canvas
is what Prezi calls the workspace you use for building your presentation.

Move around the Canvas

1. Click on the *Home* button to center your canvas and make sure you're starting from the right position.

2. Click the object you'd like to edit.

3. Use the plus and minus buttons to zoom in and out as necessary. You can also use the roller on your mouse if you have one.

   You can also use your mouse to zoom and pan in Prezi. Press and hold the left mouse button while moving the mouse around the canvas. Use the scroll button, in the center of your mouse, to zoom into, and away from, an object.

Add Text

If you used a template, placeholders are already provided for your text based on the layout you chose. All you need to do is add the words.

1. Click <u>inside</u> the object to highlight the text boundaries. From here, select *Edit Text* to bring up the *Text Editor*.

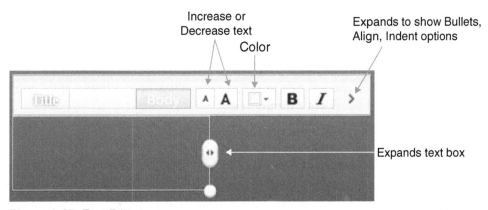

Figure 4.67 Text Editor

2. Click in the white space and type your text.

3. Click outside the text area to save your edits.

   If you want to change the look or re-format the text (align, add bullets, etc.) after you've entered it, double-click on the text to bring up the *Text Editor* again. Centering text, changing font styles, and color are all done from this text box as well. Using variety in text sizing can help your audience distinguish between main topic ideas and other details; it also can help you develop the hierarchy for your content—the larger the text, the greater the emphasis.

Manipulate Objects

▼ Transformation Tool
a set of manipulation tools that can alter, resize, move, rotate, or delete objects and text

Once you have added objects, you will likely need to edit them. To do that, you will use the **Transformation Tool**, a set of manipulation tools that can alter, resize, move, rotate, or delete objects and text (formerly the *Transformation Zebra*). This tool will appear slightly differently depending on whether you select a text box or a graphic.

Figure 4.68 Transformation Tool

Right-clicking on any object will bring up another menu with even more functions as shown in Figure 4.69. The majority of these functions work in a similar manner across most software programs.

Frames

▼ Frames
are similar to slides and a key component of Prezi. Frames can be used to add structure to your content and organize information in groups.

For example, if you have a Prezi about wines, you can organize the information into two groups—red and white—and then use frames to separate these two groups. The advantage of grouping and putting your Prezi together in frames is to reduce the chance of motion sickness in your audience when you give the presentation. If your objects are in a frame, Prezi moves more easily from object to object as opposed to randomly flying around the canvas. There are two ways to create frames: One method is to add a frame from the side bar on the left of your canvas (Figure 4.70). A second method is to use the *Insert -> Layouts* option which is covered in a later section.

1. From the left side of your canvas, click on the frame at the top and select your frame type.

2. Drag it onto the canvas. Circle and square frames are available in the free version of *Prezi*.

You can insert frames from previously added content as well.

1. Select *Insert -> My Content. . ..*

2. Choose *From Prezis* and you will see frames you've created before.

3. Click and drag the frame onto the canvas. Prezi will automatically adjust the content to match your current theme.

Figure 4.69 Additional Object Functions

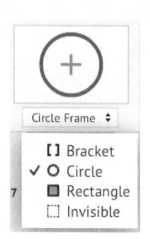

Figure 4.70 Frames Menu

A new path point will be added to your *Presentation Path*. Be sure to place it where you would like it to appear in your presentation, or remove it if you plan on later building a frame.

Every element in a frame will automatically be grouped together. This is a way to control your presentation much like controlling one slide at a time in Power Point. Moving, scaling, or rotating the frame will apply to all objects in the frame.

Use Invisible Frames

You can use invisible frames to organize your content without the additional visual weight of the frame itself. This is ideal for highlighting details on a large image, or block of text. Invisible frames are displayed during *Edit* mode, but hidden during your presentation (*Present* mode). Also, invisible frames do not group the contents, so individual objects can be moved, scaled, or rotated separately.

Note: If you will use a projector to display your Prezi, be aware of the aspect ratio difference between a laptop and a projector. Most newer laptops have a wide-screen monitor, but projectors have 4:3 aspect ratio. To see what your Prezi will look like when projected, you'll need to draw your frames with the same 4:3 ratio. To use a 4:3 ratio, hold down the *Shift* key while you are adding a frame. More specific instructions for differing aspect rations can be found at http://prezi.com/learn/aspect-ratio-guide/.

Without using a frame, you can still group content together in other ways.

Group Content Together

Often it will be useful to group multiple objects together, so they can be manipulated as a single object. For example, if you have text that is a label for an image or an object, you may want to group these things together, so that when you rotate or scale one, the other object is also manipulated as well.

Figure 4.71 Group Objects

1. Click on the first object you wish to add to a group. The object border will be highlighted.

2. While holding down the *Shift* key, click on all other objects that you wish to add to the group. This will add a box around all the items you select.

3. Click the *Group* icon at the top to group the objects together.

To *Ungroup*, first select the group, then select *Ungroup*.

2. Inserting Pictures and Objects

Now you are ready to add content to your canvas. If you used a template as the basis for your Prezi, many objects have already been added, but you will likely need to add your own specific elements as well.

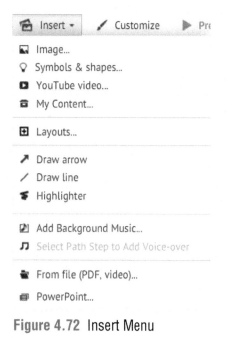

Figure 4.72 Insert Menu

Insert image   ×

Figure 4.73 Insert Images

Inserting objects, as well as many other functions, is accomplished using the *Insert* menu at the top of your screen (Figure 4.72). From here you can add images, symbols and shapes, arrows and highlights, music, and PowerPoint slides. This section covers the basics of adding Images, and Shapes. The next section includes adding Themes, Media, and PowerPoint slides to enhance your presentation.

Insert Images

1. Select *Image. . .* from the *Insert* menu.

   This will bring up the options shown in Figure 4.73

   Several images appear, but if you choose "*Search. . .*" using "*Search images on . . ..,*" Prezi can perform a Google image search. If you choose to "*Select files. . .*" you can search files on your computer.

2. Double click on the image or file you want, either from the web or your computer.

   Your image will appear on the canvas. (If you searched from the web, multiple images will appear for you to choose among. Double click on the one you want to use.)

   Be sure you have the appropriate copyright permission for the image you intend to you use. If you are searching for images from the web, we recommend you select the filter that only displays images for commercial use (Figure 4.74).

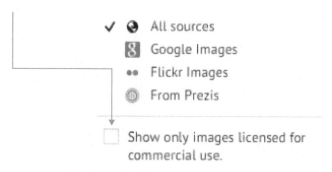

Figure 4.74 Commercial Use

3. A circle may appear to indicate that your image is downloading. Once the download is complete, click on your picture to move it wherever you'd like.

4. Use the *Transformation Tool,* to resize or reformat as necessary.

Crop an Image

If your image is larger than you need, you can crop it.

1. Double-click on an image to display the control points (on the corners).

2. Drag the control points to select the part of the image you want to keep.

3. Click anywhere outside the image to crop or use the ESC key.

Cropped parts are not permanently cropped, they are just hidden. Double-clicking the image again shows the entire, original image in case you need to start over.

Insert Symbols and shapes

Currently Prezi allows you to insert over 200 symbols and ten different shapes. These shapes, along with the line tool, can be combined in any form to create the graphic you need for your content. Prezi offers pre-designed layouts for commonly used shape combinations. There is more on this in *Enhancing your Prezi*.

1. Select *Symbols & shapes. . .* from the *Insert* menu. This will bring up the style options shown in Figure 4.75.

2. Choose the coloring/display style you'd like for your symbol or shape.

   This will bring up a second menu of options for various symbols to use.

3. Double-click on the option you wish to use. Your shape will appear in the middle of your canvas. You can then resize or move it using the *Transformation Tool*.

Add an Arrow

Suppose you want to add an arrow (other than from the Shapes menu) to show that one step leads to the next step in a process.

1. Select *Draw arrow* from the *Insert* menu.

2. Click on the canvas where you want the arrow to appear and drag to the desired length.

3. Once you let go of the mouse, a *Transformation Tool* will appear which offers thickness and color options (Style).

   Notice that the arrow has three "control points" —beginning, middle, and end.

4. Click on the beginning and end points to change the length of your arrow.

5. Click and drag on the middle control point to change the curvature of your arrow.

6. To edit the width, click on the arrow to bring up the *Transformation Tool* and use the thickness buttons to manipulate the width.

Figure 4.75 Symbols and Shapes Styles Menu

Figure 4.76 Arrow Options

Figure 4.77 Arrow Width Options

Theme

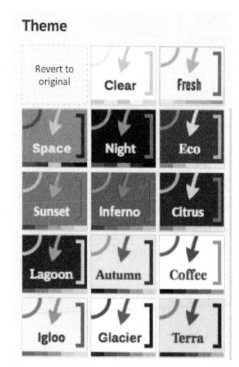

Figure 4.78 Themes Menu

▼ **Themes**
are pre-designed colors in templates that can be used to customize your Prezi presentation.

3. Enhancing your Prezi

The previous section provided instructions to help get you started with Prezi and insert text, images, and shapes. In this section, we cover how to use additional Prezi tools to give you more control over your content and create a more dynamic and engaging presentation.

Use Themes

When you select a template as the foundation for your presentation, certain colors will automatically be assigned to the background and any text or objects you add. If you would like to change any of these pre-designed colors, use *Themes* from the *Customize* menu."

You can choose a file from your computer of one of the pre-designed themes. Whatever theme you select will apply to all objects on your canvas.

Use Theme Wizard

If you would like to change any individual component of the theme, such as the background or text colors, you use the *Theme Wizard*.

To change colors:

1. Open the *Customize* menu. This brings up the *Themes* menu (Figure 4.78)

2. Select *Advanced* at the bottom of the *Themes box*. This brings up the *Theme Wizard* menu shown in Figure 4.79.

3. Select *Wizard* in the bottom left corner and Use the *Next* button to scroll through the various option to choose a new color for any part you'd like to change.

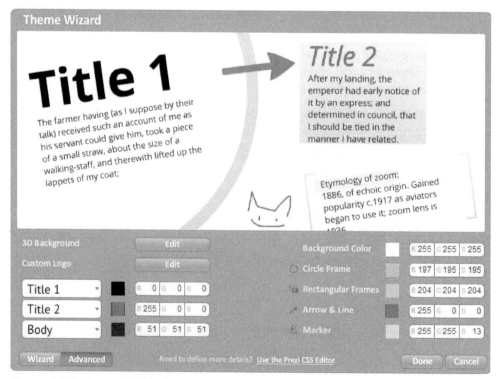

Figure 4.79 Themes Wizard

Your changes will immediately apply to the elements in the window.

To add a 3D background:

1. From the *Themes* menu shown above, select *Wizard at the bottom*.

2. Click on the *3D Background Upload* box.

3. Double-click on the image you would like to use as the background. You will see a message indicating that your image is uploading. When it's complete, you're image will appear in the *Upload* box.

4. Click *Done* when you're finished. The 3D effect is handled automatically.

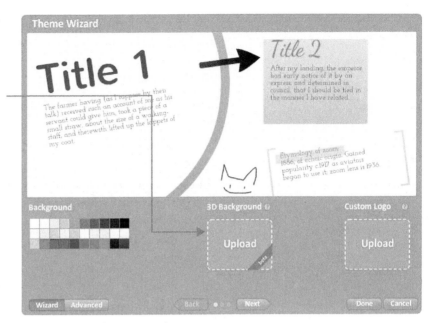

Figure 4.80 3D Background

You can zoom into and out of different parts of your image. You can add up to three 3D images in one Prezi using the *Advanced* button in the *Theme Wizard*. With multiple images, the backgrounds will fade automatically, as you zoom in and out.

To delete a 3D background:

1. Open the *Customize* menu to display the *Themes* menu.

2. Select *Advanced*.

3. Click on the red "X" in the top right corner of the 3D Background image.

4. Click *Done* when you're finished. The image will be removed from the background of your workspace.

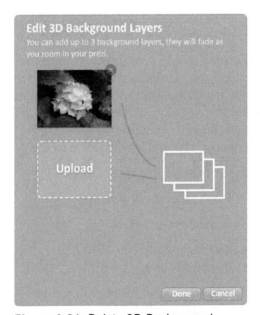

Figure 4.81 Delete 3D Background

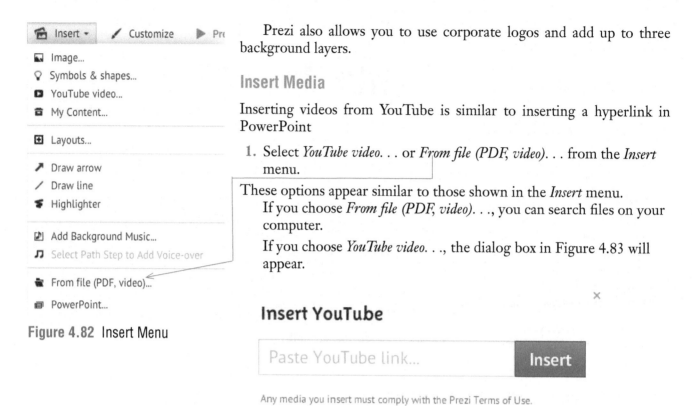

Figure 4.82 Insert Menu

Prezi also allows you to use corporate logos and add up to three background layers.

Insert Media

Inserting videos from YouTube is similar to inserting a hyperlink in PowerPoint

1. Select *YouTube video. . .* or *From file (PDF, video). . .* from the *Insert* menu.

These options appear similar to those shown in the *Insert* menu.

If you choose *From file (PDF, video). . .*, you can search files on your computer.

If you choose *YouTube video. . .*, the dialog box in Figure 4.83 will appear.

Figure 4.83 Insert YouTube content

2. Paste the URL of a YouTube content into the dialog box (not the YouTube embed code).

3. Select *Insert*.

The video will begin automatically once you reach this object in your presentation sequence.

Note: The *FLV* (Adobe Flash video file) format works best in Prezi and many free video conversion packages are available. The *AVI* is unstable at the time of publication. Beware of file size limits.

Add Audio

In many cases you may want to add sound to your presentation. Audio is particularly useful for prezis that may be embedded in a website or play continuously. Prezi audio works best when shown online without a presenter.

Audio can be added in two ways: either as background music or to specific steps in your path. In the second scenario, the sound will begin when you reach that step in the path sequence and end as you move to the next step.

To add background sound to a presentation:

1. In *Edit* mode, select *Insert* from the top menu.

2. Select the *Add Background Music. . .*

3. From your computer, select the file you want to use. You will see a message indicating that the file is uploading.

4. Once the upload is complete, you will something like Figure 4.84.
   You can click the Play button or click *Done* to continue editing your prezi.

The background music will play continuously when you are in *Present* mode. Use the trashcan icon to delete the sound from this path step.

Figure 4.84 Background sound

Note: If you have video on this path step, the background track will stop playing to allow the video sound to be heard.

To add sound to a path step:

1. Select the path step where you would like to add audio.

2. From the *Insert* menu, select *Add Voice-over to Path Step. . .* You can also right-click on the path step and select *Add Voice-over to Path Step. . .*

3. From your computer, select the file you want to use. You will see a message indicating that the file is uploading.

4. You can click the *Play* button or click *Done* to continue editing your prezi. Adding sound to a path step will trigger the *Play* and *Mute* buttons to appear when in *Present* mode.

At the time of this printing, Prezi supports the following audio formats: MP3, M4A, FLAC, WMA, WAV, OGG, AAC, 3GP. For more information on which software applications you can use to create these kinds of files, consult the online manual.

Insert PowerPoint Slides

If you'd like to use any slides you've already created in PowerPoint, you can bring those directly into Prezi. For example, you may have created a pie chart, or line graph from an Excel spreadsheet and want to use it as part of your Prezi.

1. Select "*PowerPoint. . .*" from the *Insert* menu. This will bring up a window for you to search your computer for the PowerPoint file you want to include.

2. Double-click on the file you want to use. This action will bring up a sidebar to the right of your canvas. Prezi will convert and download your PowerPoint file and display the slides in the sidebar.

3. Click on the slide you wish to use and drag it to your canvas. Drop it where you'd like it to appear.

You may lose some formatting, but most objects will come in as they were displayed in PowerPoint. You then can alter the content as you would any Prezi object. Note: Heavily animated files may come in as a separate slide for each part of the animation, but you can import the PPT animation as a video.

You can also *Insert All* of your slides at once; *Prezify* them by grouping the information into content clusters and using sizing to indicate hierarchy of ideas. (Go to http://prezi.com/pptimport/ to watch a video of the steps to *Prezify* a PowerPoint file.)

Layouts

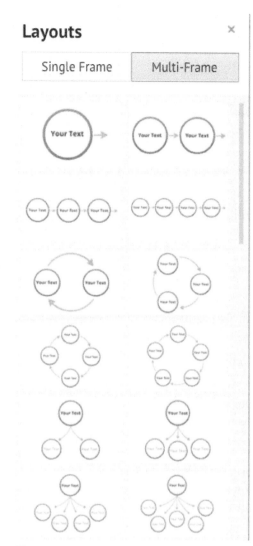

Figure 4.85 Insert a Layout

▼ Path
A path is the order in which your objects will be displayed during *Present* mode

Insert a Layout

In some cases, you may want to use a pre-designed layout to help express your idea. The *Insert Layout* (See Figure 4.85) option allows you to choose the layout that best displays your content. You can build your layout one frame at a time (Single Frame) or the Multi-Frame option provides pre-designed diagrams. This includes timelines and other formats to help your audience see and interpret your information. Here's how:

1. Select *Layouts. . .* from the *Insert* menu. This will bring up the illustration shown in Figure 4.85.

2. Select the visual layout the best represents your content.

3. Click in your diagram to begin adding content.

The objects are automatically grouped (with a *Hidden* frame—Presented in more detail in the next section) so that any change in size or rotation applies to all of the objects. However, if necessary and more useful, you can select and edit any of the objects individually.

4. Creating Your Presentation Path

Now that you have placed all of your content (text and objects) onto your canvas, you need to know how to move from one object to the next during your presentation. In PowerPoint, this movement of objects is referred to as animation, but in Prezi, it's called a *Path*. A **path** is the order in which your objects will be displayed during *Present* mode. An effective path is one that has a balance between broad overviews and small details. As we said earlier, using *Frames* to group similar content will be helpful to achieve the right balance and prevent motion sickness in your audience. During your presentation, you can take "detours" from you path at any time, in response to your audience's needs.

Create a Path

1. Zoom out until you can see all of the objects you wish to show at one time. The starting view is a full overview of the entire canvas and this "stop" will already be visible on the *Left Sidebar*

2. Click *Edit Path* at the bottom of the *Left Sidebar*. The background will change to dark gray and a thumbnail will appear in the sidebar for each object you select.

3. Click and drag the Path Point to the location in the *Sidebar* that represents the order you want it to appear (Figure 4.86). The path views shown on the *Sidebar* are similar to the sequence of slides in PowerPoint.

4. If an object does not yet have a Path Point on the *Edit Path* sequence, simply click the object on the canvas to add it to the end of the *Path Sidebar* sequence.

If you need to edit any of the objects as you are creating the path, you'll need to select *Edit Path* again to switch back to *Edit* mode (the background will change to light gray).

- To **Delete** a *Path Point*, hover over the top right edge of the thumbnail and press the red "X" button.

- To **Rearrange** the order of your path, drag and drop your thumbnails within the sidebar.

- To **Insert a new path point** between two existing path points, drag the small plus symbol (found directly after each path point on the canvas) onto the object you wish to insert

- To **Change** what the path point is linked to, drag the large numbered circle onto other objects.

- To **Capture** your current view, choose *Add current view* from the Sidebar. This will **add** it to the end of your path and you can rearrange it as necessary.

- To **View** your path in *Present mode*, click *Present* at the bottom right corner of your canvas.

- To **Delete** all of the Path points, select the *Clear All* button at the bottom of the *Sidebar*.

When your path is complete, your canvas should look similar to the one shown in Figure 4.87. The numbered sequence is the order in which your content will progress.

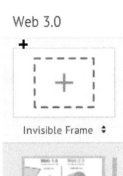

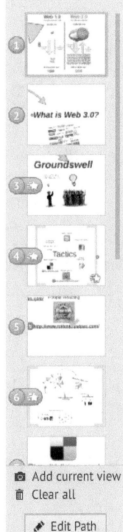

Figure 4.86
Presentation Path

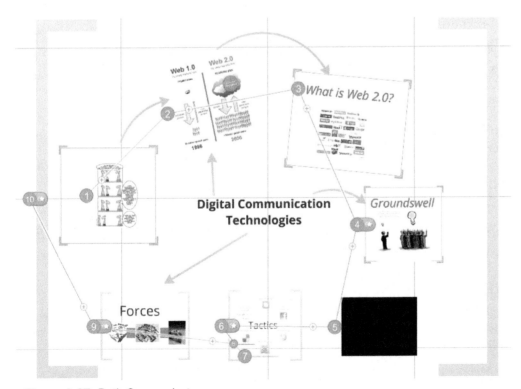

Figure 4.87 Path Screenshot

Discard animations

Preview animations

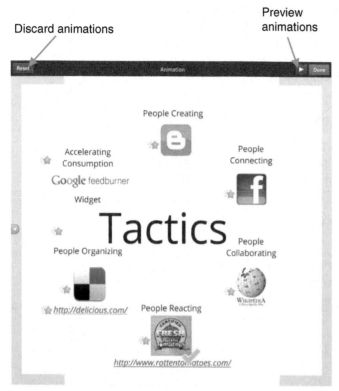

Figure 4.88 Fade in Animation

Add Fade-in Animation

Once you have designed your path, you may want some of your content to fade-in one object at a time, instead of zooming in all at once. *Fade-in Animation* works like a path step and allows you to fade-in content within a frame.

1. Make sure the frame is already in place around your content and you are in *Edit* mode.

2. Select the *Animation* icon to the left of your thumbnail (in the shape of a star). This will open the *Animation* window.

   If you don't see a "star" or some other symbol beside your path number, you are likely not in *Edit* mode.

3. Click on each object, in the order you'd like it to appear. As you do this, you will see numbered green stars appear to indicate the order of appearance.

4. Click *Done* when you are finished animating objects.

You can **preview** the fade-in effect by pressing the *Play* button at the top of the Animation window.

To **remove** a single animation, hover over the star and click the red "x" to delete the effect. You can also use the *Reset* button at the top to delete all effects and start over.

If you have used *Hidden* frames, or have several objects you'd like to fade-in together, you'll need to *Group* them.

Presenting Your Prezi

You have created and edited your content, so now it's time to actually present your Prezi.

Switch to *Present* Mode

1. Click the *Present* button at the top of your canvas (Figure 4.89). This automatically places you in *Present* mode and shows your Prezi in full screen.

2. Use the arrow keys on your keyboard to move back and forth in your Prezi (according to the path you set previously).

Additional options in the bottom right corner are shown in Figure 4.90.

When you are in *Present* mode, all other menus hide automatically to give you a clean backdrop. You can return to *Edit* mode at any time by pressing the ESC key or the pencil icon in the top right corner.

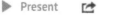   Present ⤴ ⚙ ❓ ✕ Exit

Figure 4.89 Present Button

Autoplay  Fullscreen

Figure 4.90 Presentation Options

Use a Remote Clicker

If you plan to use a remote clicker during the presentation (which we recommend so you aren't tied to the computer), below are the instructions for moving forward in your presentation and how to zoom.

1. Be sure you have created your path.

2. Install the latest version of Adobe Flash Player (get the latest version from: http://get.adobe.com/flashplayer)

3. Select *Present* mode.

4. Once you enter Present mode, click the *Allow* button at the top of the screen.

   You can move forward or backward using the arrow keys, and zoom in and out using the up and down arrow keys. If your remote does not already work this way, you can reconfigure it. For specific configuration instructions for different remotes, using smartphone apps, or if you are having trouble using your clicker, go to https://prezi.com/support/article/presenting/presenting-with-remote-clickers/?lang=en.

Download Your Prezi

In cases where you might not have Internet access, you will need to download and save your Prezi to your laptop. Knowing how to create a portable copy of your presentation also makes it easy to send to conference organizers or your listeners after your presentation (even if they don't have a Prezi account), or create a CD or DVD.

1. Go to Prezi.com.

2. Click on *Your prezis* and select the one you want to download.

3. Select *Download from the options beneath your file.*

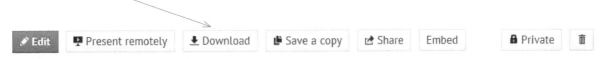

Figure 4.91 File Options Bar

This will bring up the window shown in Figure 4.92

Figure 4.92 Download Options

4. Click on *Download*.

You will see a window that indicates your Prezi is being created. Note for Windows users: file names that are too long may not open.

5. When the download is complete, click on the *Open* prompt in the download window. *Prezi* will create a zipped file. Windows users: file names that are too long may not open.

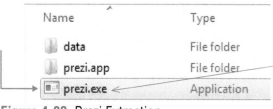

6. Double click on the zipped folder.

7. Click on *Prezi.exe* to load your portable Prezi file.

8. A dialog box opens to unzip the files. Click on *Extract all* to open all other necessary files.

Figure 4.93 Prezi Extraction

9. Select the destination folder for your Prezi. Click *OK*.

10. Select *Extract*.

11. Go to your destination folder and you will see the *prezi.exe* file.

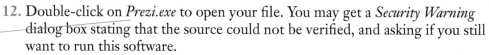

12. Double-click on *Prezi.exe* to open your file. You may get a *Security Warning* dialog box stating that the source could not be verified, and asking if you still want to run this software.

Figure 4.94 prezi.exe

Your Prezi should open in a new window.

Notes: Embedded YouTube videos will not work without Internet access. Also, portable Prezis cannot be edited. To edit your Prezi, got to prezi.com, make changes, and download again.

Use Autoplay

Depending on your situation and purpose, you may want to set your Prezi to play automatically or even loop through repeatedly.

1. Be sure you have created your path.

2. Select *Present* to bring up the presentation controls.

3. At the bottom of your screen, hover over the arrow to display the timing options.

4. Select the interval you want to use.

Figure 4.95 Autoplay Options

To stop the Autoplay, press either the back or forward arrows.

Print your Prezi

You may want a hard copy of your Prezi to use as notes or to keep for future reference.

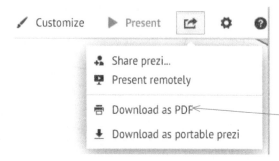

1. Open your Prezi.

2. Make sure you have created a path.

3. Click the Share icon in the upper right hand corner of your canvas. Select *Download* as PDF.

4. Prezi will begin paginating your path and create a pdf file. Prezi will create the same number of pages as there are path

Figure 4.96 Print Prezi

points in your Prezi plus an overview page of the whole canvas view, so you might want to limit the number of path points.

When the pagination is complete, the prompt will change.

5. Select *Save PDF.* This action will bring up a browser window for you to name and save your file.

6. Locate this file and print it out as you would any .pdf file.

6. Sharing Your Prezi

Prezi offers several options to view and edit your presentation in collaboration with others. This feature can be especially useful for students working on a group project or virtual team members who find it hard to meet with one another or are located in different parts of the world. You can allow others to edit the presentation simultaneously with you (up to 10 at a time), or send it to them to edit on their own time. All users must have a Prezi account.

Invite to Edit

1. Click the *Share* icon from the shortcuts menu,

2. Select *Share prezi . . .* which brings up the box in Figure 4.97.

3. Copy this link and send it to whoever you'd like to participate. You can also type the email address of anyone you'd like to have access. A message below will confirm that an email has been sent.

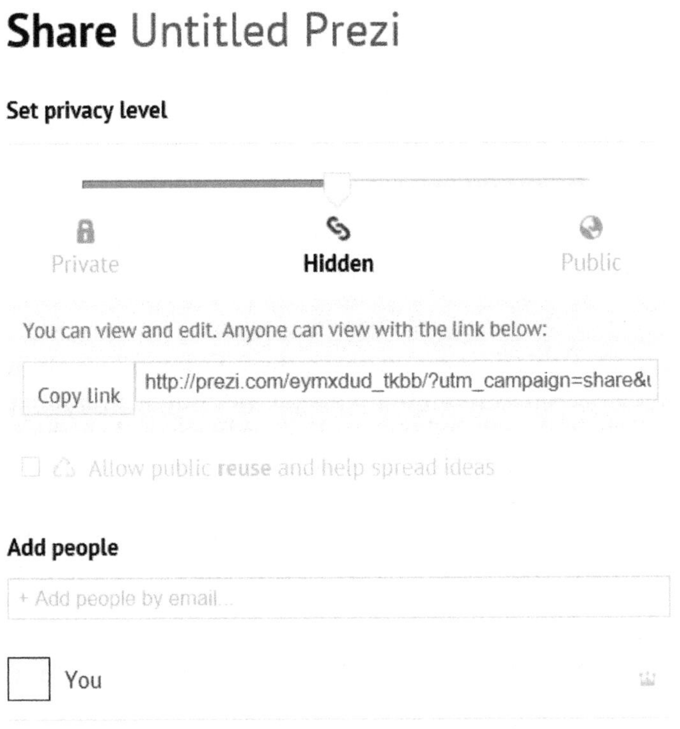

Share Untitled Prezi

Set privacy level

| Private | Hidden | Public |

You can view and edit. Anyone can view with the link below:

| Copy link | http://prezi.com/eymxdud_tkbb/?utm_campaign=share&u |

☐ Allow public **reuse** and help spread ideas

Add people

+ Add people by email...

☐ You

Figure 4.97 Invite to Edit

▼ Avatar
refers to the graphical
representation that
participants choose for
themselves.

When the recipient opens the link, you will see the viewer's avatar in the sidebar on the right hand side of your canvas. As in online games, *Avatar* refers to the graphical representation that participants choose for themselves. All collaborators can edit the content of the canvas simultaneously. If you want to show your Prezi to someone online but don't want them to have editing capability, you can use *Present online*.

Present Remotely

When you're ready to present your Prezi, click on the *Share* icon and select *Present remotely* to start your presentation. This brings up Figure 4.98.

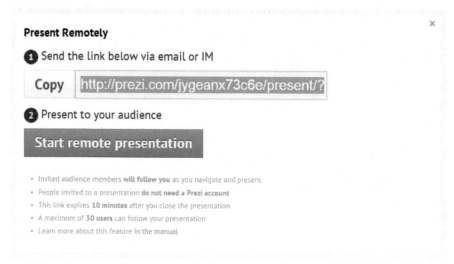

Figure 4.98 Present Remotely

This same capability, *Present remotely* can also be accessed from the *Options* bar when you open your Prezi.

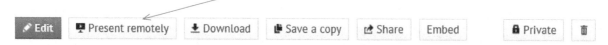

Figure 4.99 File *Options Bar*

When others open this link, you will see their avatar. They can watch as you present, but can't edit. A maximum of 30 people can watch a remote presentation at the same time. The link will expire ten minutes after you close the presentation.

Give Control

Occasionally, you may want to hand over online control of the presentation to someone else. Here's how.

1. Click on the co-collaborator's avatar, which brings up several options.

2. Click on *Hand over presentation* to allow your co-collaborator to take control of the presentation. A message appears indicating your collaborator is now presenting.

You can still explore freely by clicking on your own avatar and selecting *Explore freely*.

Privacy Settings

Once you have created a Prezi, you might want to others to use it as a template for their own presentations. Your privacy choices are dependent upon which Prezi plan you have. The original version of your Prezi it not editable, but others can make a copy to modify for their own use.

Public Plan Holders:

Prezis are automatically public but you can allow your prezi to be reused by others. This is especially helpful, if you've created a useful path sequence or incorporated unusual video or audio that others might want to model.

Enjoy, EDU Enjoy, Pro, and EDU Pro Plan Holders:

The privacy state is controlled with a slider that appears when you select the Share icon. Drag the slider icon to set your prezi as Public.

The privacy settings box will change to reflect the new settings. Making your Prezi public will place it in the *Explore* database for anyone with a Prezi account to see. Search engines will index it, and others can comment on it.

Prezi definitely gives you more flexibility in designing and creating visual supplements for presentations. Many speakers have used Prezi with great success, but just as many have gone overboard with new features, like zooming in and out, at will. As we've said several times before, but it bears repeating, only use those features that truly enhance your message. Don't put in a rotation, or a path point, or zoom to every item—just because you can. As with any other tool, don't let Prezi overwhelm you, the speaker.

vtionships between your main points and choose the design layout that best suits your content. Once you have decided on the layout that best suits your purpose, you may find Prezi easier to use. In the box below, a speaker at our university, who uses Prezi quite successfully, gives you some useful tips and tricks.

BOX 4.1

PREZI—TIPS AND TRICKS

Prezi is a fantastic visual aid tool, which offers presenters the ability to add visual interest, spatial interactivity, and flexibility in design beyond that of other presentation supplements. Perhaps its best accomplishment is Prezi's ability to move away from linear thought and demonstrate relationships between and among ideas. This achievement, however, can also become something of a handicap. Here are some ideas to consider when actually creating your next Prezi.

Think Aesthetically

Begin your Prezi by developing a larger image, one which is pleasing to the eye and provides greater understanding of your presentation. Then, consider where it would make sense to visually include subpoints. Use the zoom function to place smaller frames for detailed ideas, grouped together by theme. Think of the overall Prezi as a single image with sub-elements or images on which you focus in the presentation.

(Continued)

BOX 4.1 (continued)

Offer Orientation

Provide your audience with orienting reference points throughout the presentation. These should be locations on your presentation path that offer a meaningful overview for part or all of your presentation. Further, they should be visual references. Make each point brief in length and large in size, then use them to orient and focus listeners/viewers' attention, as you present. Start from and return to these points regularly.

Keep the Keys Hot

Learn keyboard shortcuts for better control of your presentation. Shortcuts can be activated by selecting the *Options* tab and clicking "*On*" under *Enable shortcuts*. Once activated, the space bar will now activate presentation mode. From here, a variety of shortcuts can be used, both in and out of presentation mode. For help with this technique, go to: https://prezi.zendesk.com/entries/22628787-keyboard-shortcuts.

Think Outside the Zoom

Scale can used to demonstrate hierarchical relations. Rotation can be interesting and draw in audiences. Using Prezi's ability to leave the path and easily return—by simply clicking on the Path Point—can allow for audience interaction. But don't overdo it. Like any presentation aid, Prezi is just an aid. Be sure you are using it to maintain attention, not simply to offer visual distractions.

Finally, have fun. Play with the program—it's the best way to learn.

Jeremy Remy
University of Colorado–*Colorado Springs*

EXERCISES TO IMPROVE YOUR PREZI

Exercises specific to Prezi are more difficult than exercises for PPT because the two tools are distinctly different. Some of the options available in PPT are not available in Prezi and vice versa. Additionally, Prezi integrates many functions whereas PPT has more distinct and separate steps to create certain layouts or effects. However, two of the exercises offered in the PowerPoint section are shown below.

1. The image below shows bullet points indicating an historical series of events.

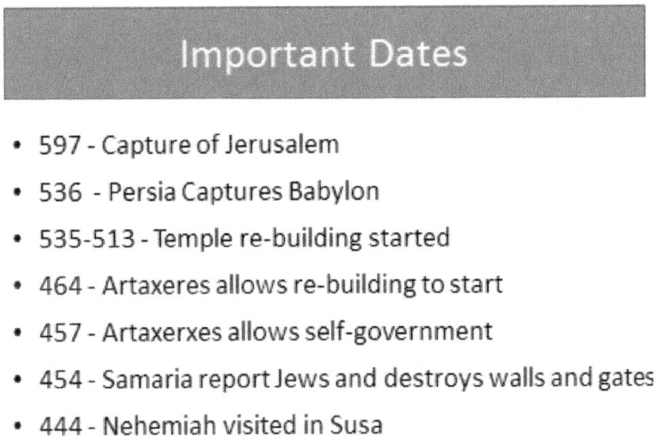

Important Dates
• 597 - Capture of Jerusalem
• 536 - Persia Captures Babylon
• 535-513 - Temple re-building started
• 464 - Artaxeres allows re-building to start
• 457 - Artaxerxes allows self-government
• 454 - Samaria report Jews and destroys walls and gates
• 444 - Nehemiah visited in Susa

Figure 4.100 Bulltet Points

You realize this is a bit bland, so you want to add some "movement" to the slide. Your first instinct might be to:

a. Put these dates/bullets into separate frames so you can zoom into them one at a time (CAUTION: Don't get too carried away with "zooming").

Although you have added "movement, the view is still very "text heavy" and still BORING. If you try to apply **Visualization** to this content, you realize the text represents a timeline.

b. Convert these bullet points, into some sort of timeline that displays the events more pictorially.

Be sure to sequence your Presentation Path in the proper order

Temple Re-building started 535-515
Artaxerxes allows self-government 457
Capture of Jerusalem 597
Nehemiah visited in Susa 444
600 BC
400 BC
536 Persia Captures Babylon
464 Artaxeres allows re-building to start
454 Samaria reports Jews and destroys walls and gates

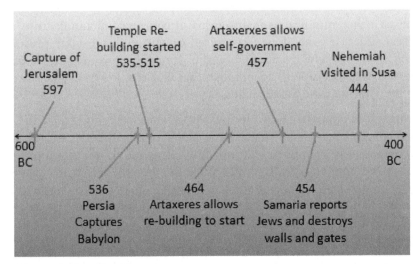

Figure 4.101 Timeline

This might be okay, but experiment with adding actual images and using various zoom in and zoom out features to provide the audience with both an overall view and in-depth content. This is one of the features that makes Prezi so unique.

2. Search the Internet to determine the adoption process for your local Humane Society or pet shelter. Build an illustration to display the sequence of steps. Use the Zoom feature to offer both an overview of the process as well as further detail for each specific step.

   Creating these presentations, using both PowerPoint and Prezi, will give you a good idea of how you can accomplish the same outcome using two very different types of presentation software.

OUR FINAL THOUGHTS ABOUT PREZI, POWERPOINT, AND *PUBLIC SPEAKING 3.0*

We now close our discussion of this part of ours book with a few summative ideas that we've picked up by actually using and teaching others to use the dynamic, new presentation tools available today. We base these recommendations on an interesting notion purported by early Greek philosophers as well as some writers of modern fiction. These wise minds tell us that our primary personal characteristic, our primary virtue, foreshadows or points to our fatal or primary flaw. The fatal flaw is a positive trait carried to the extreme (thrifty becomes miserly; courageous becomes reckless, and protective becomes overbearing). So you ask, how does this philosophical notion relate to today's presentation technology? Indeed, technology's primary virtue, its capacity to do so much, may point to some of its primary flaws. For example:

■ Because Prezi, for example, is capable of doing so much, the instructions for its use may appear complicated. As a result, it's harder to learn to use than other presentation software programs. The real problem with this flaw is that you may take time away from preparing and visualizing the content of your presentation (See "visualizing" in Part II) and devote that time to learning how to prezi—yes, that is now a verb.

■ Because of the complicated instructions, it can be challenging to print a set of Prezi slides, if a handout is required or will enhance your presentation. Although we gave you instructions earlier for printing your prezi, none of our students have been able to accomplish that task easily, which takes away from their preparation time for speeches.

■ Perhaps most important—all the new presentation technologies are capable of amazing effects—and that virtue does point directly to the flaw of overcomplicating your presentation. The zooms and fly-ins appear more like a television commercial or a live billboard at the football field than a professional presentation. The listeners' attention is drawn to the "wow" effect of the zoom or fly-in. The *Simplicity* principle says that may distract from you as a speaker and the details in your carefully crafted message.

It appears we have come full circle regarding the creation of presentations, back to the simple premises discussed in Parts I, II, and III of this book:

1. Our society is now more "visual."

2. If we want be effective presenters, we need to apply the basic design principles espoused by experts in Vision Science.

3. We need to master, or at least become fairly proficient at, using presentation software.

We hope you found our advice helpful, particularly when you use software tools like PowerPoint and Prezi. Remember, no matter what bells and whistles may come with your software, you should always practice the five techniques of our *SCRAP Approach*: *Simplicity*, *Contrast*, *Repetition*, *Alignment*, and *Proximity*. Let us know how it goes for you, we would be glad to hear from you!

Now, in Part V, we'll discuss how to deliver your presentations most effectively, using a different set of hardware and software tools.

GLOSSARY

Avatar refers to the graphical representation of a participant usually found in online games, virtual worlds, chat rooms, or other online communities.

Bar charts display data bars that are positioned horizontally.

Canvas is the term Prezi uses to describe the workspace for building your presentation.

Chartjunk refers to any visual element on a chart or graph that isn't necessary to the audience's understanding of the data.

Column charts represent data using bars that are positioned vertically.

Cloud-based applications are software accessed using a web browser, but the actual software, data, and files are stored at a remote location.

Explode refers to separating the segments of a pie chart from one another.

Hyperlinks allow you to jump to another location, either within the software or outside the application, based on the location or address you specify.

Path is the order in which your objects will be displayed during *Show* mode.

Slide Master is a single governing slide that establishes all of your color and font choices to maintain continuity across your slides.

Self-running presentations are presentations that don't require a speaker.

Templates are a series of slides in which all of the design elements are established for you, including object positioning, font and color choices as well as various patterned backgrounds.

Transformation Toolbox is a set of manipulation tools that are used to alter, resize, move, rotate, or delete objects and text.

Delivering 21st Century Presentations

Once you have created your slides or other visual aids, then it's time to think about the actual delivery of your speech or presentation. In Part I, we presented the eight competencies of an effective speech. Parts II, III, and IV addressed how the first four competencies can be enhanced by creating high quality, impactful visuals. In this final part, we address the major role of emerging technologies and tools in actually delivering 21st century presentations. Table 5.1 describes the last four of those competencies and what they look like when you deliver your speech at an excellent level. Today's wired world requires more than just learning about volume, rate, eye contact, and gestures. We must also recognize how those various physical behaviors are impacted by technology. Presentations now come in various forms. Teachers and students alike, "present" to each other in online classes. Employees will likely receive some portion of their workplace training online. A prospective job candidate may have a preliminary interview using a video conferencing tool such as Skype or GoToMeeting. All of these scenarios are forms of public speaking that require a solid understanding not just of delivery, but also how technology affects their delivery.

As with any tool, the key is to determine whether your presentation can be enhanced using technology. Because we now have so many more tools to use, that does not mean we should always use them. As happened with earlier speech aids and tools, speakers may sometimes use technology aids as a stand in for a poorly designed presentation. This would only set you up to repeat the mistakes of early PowerPoint (PPT) users. When PPT and other visual projection aids first became available, many speakers, presenters, and educators, became so enamored with the technology, that they replaced well-designed content, clear organization, and engaging delivery with whiz-bang features that soon became dull and boring. Let's not fall into that technology trap again. Adding web tools to your presentation should not take the place of effort and practice to make sure your presentation is dynamic and engaging. Effective public speaking is, and always has been, about well thought out content, delivered in an interesting and engaging manner.

TABLE 5.1 The Competent Public Speaker Delivery Competencies

The Four Competencies	Delivery at an Excellent Level
Uses language appropriate to the audience & occasion.	The speaker uses language that is exceptionally clear, vivid, and appropriate.
Uses vocal variety in rate, pitch, and intensity (volume) to heighten and maintain interest appropriate to the audience & occasion.	The speaker makes exceptional use of vocal variety in a conversational mode.
Uses pronunciation, grammar, and articulation appropriate to the audience & occasion.	The speaker has exceptional articulation, pronunciation, and grammar.
Uses physical behaviors that support the verbal message.	The speaker demonstrates exceptional posture, gestures, bodily movement, facial expressions, eye contact, and use of dress.

That basic principle hasn't changed, norneither should it. But technology has transformed what audiences expect as well as what speakers need to do before, during, and after a presentation. Understanding these two major effects will ensure you are fully prepared to be a 21st century speaker, regardless of the format or scenario.

CHANGES IN 21ST CENTURY AUDIENCES

As a result of multiple factors, including the explosion of Internet tools and software, three major changes have occurred regarding the listening audience, and these changes have a direct impact on how speakers deliver presentations. The 21st century public speaker needs to recognize that:

- Audiences Now Have Different Expectations.
- Audiences Want To Talk Back.
- Audiences Are Not Always in the Same Room.

Audiences Now Have Different Expectations

Audiences have changed in the last 20 years, and their expectations are quite high. Although there are likely many factors to explain this increase in listener expectations, three are most relevant to our discussion. First, as we mentioned in Part III, the increase in Internet tools available to almost anyone means expertise in digital media no longer resides solely in the hands of "professionals." A simple search of the Internet uncovers many free software tools and applications the average person can use to create high quality multimedia presentations on his/her own. Therefore, audiences now expect speakers to include high quality, multimedia as a part of a presentation.

A second contributing factor centers on audiences' interconnectedness. The majority of listeners have some sort of social software (multiplayer online games, blogs, bookmarking), social media account (Facebook, LinkedIn) or use technology (texting, Skype) to interact with others in their social and/or professional circles.

Image © nopporn, 2013. Used under license from Shutterstock, Inc.

Figure 5.1 The 21st Century Audience

Audiences

Increasingly, the overall population spends many hours online in connection with individuals across their social and professional realms. As a result, audiences expect speakers to include interconnected features in their presentations that facilitate interaction.

Third, the explosion of free online learning opportunities, such as Khan Academy (www.khanacademy.org), or complete online university courses such as those offered by Coursera.org (a collaboration of 33 universities including Stanford and Duke) or the combined efforts of Harvard and MIT (MITx), means the individual has access to most any type of content to teach themselves. They can probably get the information you are sharing from any number of other sources, so the traditional lecture style makes you, the speaker, somewhat irrelevant. So audiences have very high expectations for the information you do present.

Figure 5.2 Inter Connected

Audiences Want to Talk Back

A second audience shift centers on the change in the characteristics of today's audiences. Much research has been conducted on *Generation Y*, sometimes referred to as *Millennials*, the *net generation* or *digital natives*. Although there is no precise date, *Digital natives* are teens and twenty-somethings, (born after 1990) who have never known a world without the Internet, laptops, cell phones, and 24/7 connectivity. Indeed, digital natives have lots of experience with Internet tools and applications for connecting with others, sharing interests and opinions, and having their voices heard. Dobson describes the 'net generation' as a generation of young people who have grown up with the new form of empowerment that technology has offered[1]. Loy explains that Millennials are "independent thinkers and have been raised to *voice* their ideas and opinions."[2]

▼ **Digital Natives**
are teens and twenty-somethings, (born after 1990) who have never known a world without laptops, cell phones and 24/7 connectivity.

Consequently, today's listeners will expect speakers to integrate these same collaborative and social technologies to allow the listeners to "talk back" to them during presentations.

Corbin Ball, an international speaker and consultant who helps clients use technology clarifies this expectation.

> "Web 2.0 technologies now allow us to have our voice heard on blogs, online videos, social websites, online user ratings of hotels and sellers, and much more. We expect to have our voices heard online, and this will carry over to meetings. Audience participation will be increasingly demanded of speakers and meeting planners."[3]

Figure 5.3 Technology to "Talk-Back"

Cliff Atkinson, author of *The Backchannel: How Audiences are Using Twitter and Social Media and Changing Presentations Forever*, echoes this sentiment. "Audiences expect to be asked their opinion, expect to contribute to the content, expect to share experiences with others, and speakers who try to shut this down will find the numbers of listeners beginning to drop."[4]

Finally, Chris Heuer, a social media consultant in San Francisco with years of experience in conferences and meetings, foretells the impact of technology in presentations. In recounting an experience from a conference at Stanford University where a chat room conversation was displayed on a screen behind the speakers, Heuer said,

"The value in the chat room was greater than what was being said on the stage . . . People now have a voice, enabled by technology, to participate and be heard, and they're going to use it. This has only just begun. It's only the first inkling of how people are going to seize the power from institutions. People in power need to find ways to get the audience to participate."[5]

http://www.interbrand.com/Libraries/Blogs/millenials_ib.sflb.ashx

Figure 5.4 21st Century Speaking tools

Speakers who don't incorporate technology into their presentations risk losing an ever larger segment of their audience. The good news is that new tools and applications now offer speakers much more variety to interact with and engage audiences. In traditional face-to-face presentations (f2f), a speaker asks questions, polls the audience, and engages in discussion with listeners as part of the process. But, in 21st century presentations, the audience also talks back. With tools such as text messaging (SMS), Clickers, chat rooms, Twitter, BackNoise, and many others, the audience now has more opportunity to contribute to a presentation. Not only do audiences have more ways to participate, they now fully expect that speakers will welcome and encourage this participation. These increased listener expectations mean that the 21st century speaker must be prepared to integrate these tools into presentations. A 21st century audience expects a 21st century speaker.

Audiences Are Not Always in the Same Room

A third major shift affecting the speaker's delivery is the availability of platforms that allow you to speak to large and small groups all over the world, without anyone having to leave their desk. As speakers, we are no longer limited to a single room with the audience directly in front of us. The Internet, combined with many software applications, now allows a speaker to present to people in another room or listeners in another country, some of whom they may never meet face-to-face. This can be as simple as broadcasting a PowerPoint file, holding a Skype conference between two people, hosting a webinar with 20 listeners, or producing a telecast with participants all over the globe. No matter what the size of your audience, you must adjust your presentation to match the unique characteristics of the remote platform or virtual presentation.

Webinars are still one of the most common virtual presentations. A webinar is a combination of the words **web**cast and sem**inar**.

A webinar is a presentation, delivered online, using visuals, the presenter's voice, and interactive elements to bring people together in real time for training, information, and collaboration (Figure 5.5).

David Thompson, Chief Marketing Officer at WebEx Communications explains,

> "Our customers use webinars to roll out a new software product, or a new drug if they're a pharmaceutical company, or they might have a large gathering of sales people to be briefed by the marketing people on a new marketing program."[6]

▼ **Webinar**
is a combination of the words webcast and seminar. A presentation, delivered online, using visuals, the presenter's voice, and interactive elements to bring people together for training, information, and collaboration.

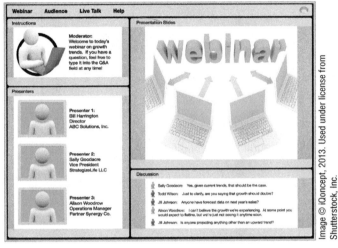

Image © iQoncept, 2013. Used under license from Shutterstock, Inc.

Figure 5.5 Webinar Concept

Even though some of the newer webinar delivery systems require a little more preparation, the eventual outcome is usually worth it. Listed below are just some of the advantages of using a webinar to deliver information:

■ Reduced Costs—It is usually much cheaper to use a virtual meeting system to reach your audience than to pay for air travel, hotels and meals.

■ Reach a larger audience—Not having travel expenses for every attendee means more people can actually participate.

■ Collaborate with participants—Most webinar platforms offer useful tools to interact and collaborate with the participants. For example, *AdobeConnect* and Blackboard *Collaborate* allow separate "breakout rooms" for small groups to meet separately, but simultaneously.

■ Connect geographically-dispersed colleagues—Webinars are a terrific way to bring industry related professionals together in a real-time environment, no matter where they are located (Figure 5.6).

Image © NarayTrace, 2013. Used under license from Shutterstock, Inc.

Figure 5.6 Webinars are not limited by geographical boundaries

Although it is hard to calculate the number of webinars presented every year, a review of industries such as pharmaceuticals, marketing and sales companies, banking, travel, and consulting companies all report the number of webinars, both offered and attended, has increased. From a survey of 10,000 webinar participants, the UK consulting firm World Trade Group. Ltd (WTG) found that 52 percent of the respondents attended two or more webinars a month7. As for why people attend a webinar, the respondents listed[8] (Figure 5.7):

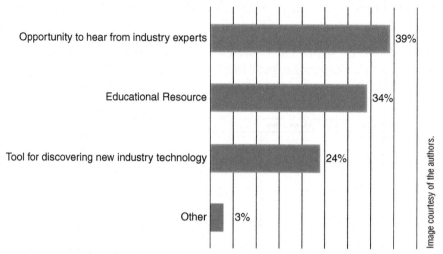

Figure 5.7 Reasons for Attending a Webinar

Despite the webinar being a valuable tool for presentations, some of the novelty has worn off. Participants' complaints often sound similar to what we hear about poor in-person presentations (Figure 5.8).

Figure 5.8 Participant complaints

- "The speaker just read from the slides."
- "There was no interaction with other participants"
- "I didn't feel comfortable asking questions"
- "I had a hard time following the speaker because the instructions weren't clear."

As with other technological advances, people were initially excited about the webinar, but they didn't really think about how they would need to change their presentations to make the most of it. But instead of dismissing webinars as a delivery option, speakers need to adapt and polish their presentation skills to make the best use of this delivery platform. Webinars continue to be effective, and particularly cost effective, when speakers adjust their delivery to match the technology.

To review, audiences have changed, as a result of technology, in three big ways—they have different expectations, they want to talk back to the speaker, and they're often not in the same room. The result of these three significant shifts is that speakers need more than just good visuals and a few questions to solicit feedback. Speakers must give audiences something they can't get *for themselves*, or *by themselves*. What many conference attendees, employees, students, and other listener groups really want is the opportunity to collaborate, network, and learn from others. Now, in addition to a visually stimulating presentation, audiences also expect polished presenters who can comfortably integrate Web 2.0 tools and applications into their presentations, and offer opportunities for listeners to contribute, participate, and share. Learning how to best manage and use the new presentation technologies is the focus of this last section of our book.

The simplest way to address both content and technical concerns associated with delivering a 21st century presentation, whether in person or remotely, as a participant or main speaker, is to divide our discussion into three phases:

- Before the Presentation
- During the Presentation
- After the Presentation

BEFORE THE PRESENTATION

Preparing presentations often can take a lot of time. Depending on how important the presentation is, you may have already spent countless hours preparing beautifully designed slides and rehearsing your content. But you can't stop there. Just a little more effort on your part will ensure the delivery of your presentation runs as smoothly as your slides. Follow the steps below to make sure you have covered all the bases to get ready for your presentation.

1. Call Your Contact.

Whether you are preparing for a virtual meeting, a video interview, or speaking at a conference, check with the person who contacted you and reconfirm the time, date, and location (if applicable). Then you can move to more technically oriented questions. Your contact may not have the specific answers you need, but he or she should be able to refer you to someone who does.

When you talk to your contact (or technical staff), ask the following questions depending on your specific situation.

If you are participating in a video conference or attending a webinar from your home or office:

- What is the link to the meeting space?
- What video conferencing software will we be using?
- Do I need specific login credentials?
- How many others will be participating?

If you are presenting outside of your home or office:

- How big is the room?
- What is the configuration of the furniture, etc.
- Will you be using a microphone? Handheld? Lavaliere?
- What version of software is loaded on the computer you will present from? (If you're not using your own laptop).
- Is the room set up for wireless access? Do you need a special password for access?
- If you're using a backchannel (such as *Twitter*), has a specific hashtag already been created for the event/content? If yes, then send a conference related tweet to the listeners to generate interest approximately one week before you speak. More on backchannels can be found in the next section.
- Who should I contact if I need further technical assistance?

▼ **Hashtag**
is a word or phrase prefixed with the symbol "#" that is a form of a metadata tag. A hashtag is commonly used to group information and link it to a searchable phrase that returns any context that includes the hashtag, for example, 21st Century Presentations.

2. Plan Your Attire with Technology in Mind.

We're sure you know how to dress appropriately for your audience and occasion, but certain equipment or projection devices can impact what you should wear. Think about the following when deciding on attire.

If you're using a microphone, what type?

- A handheld microphone is fairly common, but be cautious with your shoe choice so as not to trip on the trailing wire.
- A lapel microphone frees your hands, but think about the kind of shirt or blouse you might attach it to. Depending on the fabric, the weight of the microphone might pull on the fabric in unflattering ways. If appropriate, a suit jacket lapel is perfect for a lavaliere microphone (Figure 5.9). Also, consider whether your jewelry might cause sound depending on the location of your microphone.

If your image is being projected, make sure you don't wear something with a "busy" pattern.

- Wear solid colors or a fabric with a large pattern. Whether you're using a simple webcam attached to your computer or presenting via satellite, blouses or ties with a polka dot or checked pattern usually don't look very good when projected through a camera lens.

Image © Ruslan Rizvanov, 2012. Used under license from Shutterstock, Inc.

Figure 5.9 A lapel microphone

■ Dress with your skin color in mind. If you have dark skin, don't wear a white blouse or vice versa because the contrast is too much for the camera. In person, this high contrast looks fine, however on a projected screen, it is too bright from some angles, or washed out from other angles. Muted or lower contrast colors will provide better balance for the camera.

3. Pack the Accessories You'll Need.

There's nothing worse than showing up for a presentation and realizing you forgot your flash drive, or the power cord for your laptop. Even if you think you won't need these items, it's always good to have a backup just in case.

Be sure to take:

■ Flash Drive (and email your presentation to yourself just in case)

■ Clicker (if applicable, check the batteries)

■ Laptop and power cord

■ Notes or handouts

■ Evaluation forms

Image © zentilia, 2013. Used under license from Shutterstock, Inc.

Image © Muellek Josef, 2013. Used under license from Shutterstock, Inc.

Figure 5.10 Presentation Accessories   Image © Ensuper, 2013. Used under license from Shutterstock, Inc.

4. Practice with the Technology.

Most basic public speaking textbooks advise you to rehearse your speech and check your timing, but they usually don't say anything about practicing with the technical components you will use during your presentation. For example, beginning public speakers may be unfamiliar with various software or hardware components used to actually give a speech. Even if a student has created an effective set of slides, he or she may not have experience actually starting the slide show to begin the presentation. If the speaker is searching for the correct command to begin the slide show, or is not sure how to set the volume and looks a little lost, these uncertain behaviors will reflect negatively and affect the audience's perception of the speaker's professionalism. Before you give your presentation, if at all possible, try to practice with the hardware and software components you will actually use.

Follow these steps, so you feel confident and ready to speak:

■ Open your presentation using the hardware/software platform that you'll be using. If you are a participant, download any necessary software and check that you can log in to the meeting space.

■ Turn on the projection device/control panel to display your slides.

- Run through all slides from beginning to end.

- Stand at the back of the room and look at your slides.

- How does the resolution look from the back row?

- Will the lights be on, off, or dimmed during your presentation? How will this affect visibility and the resolution of your slides or handouts?

- Check the volume (if applicable).

- Access the Internet (if applicable).

- Check all hyperlinks, animations, and video clips to make sure they appear easily and as intended. Links to outside content may be impacted by the speed of the Internet provider or the projection device being used. Some animations run very slowly on certain systems and much faster on others. For specific problems, contact a technical staff member before you speak, not after you're actually speaking to a live audience.

- Test any *Audience Response System (ARS)* you intend to use.

Image © ariadna de raadt, 2013. Used under license from Shutterstock, Inc.

Figure 5.11 How do your slides look from the back of the room?

5. Planning for Remote/Virtual Presentations

If you are giving a remote presentation, or conducting a virtual meeting or webinar, here are the main things to consider before you speak. The following seven steps are based on a list of best practices from the *Community Sector Council of Newfoundland and Labrador (Canada)*[9] and on our own experiences as presenters and participants in remote presentations.

Step 1: Determine your platform.

A wide variety of webinar platforms are available, with more emerging all the time. *Skype, GoToWebinar, Adobe Connect, WebEx,* and *Microsoft Live Meeting* are a few of the most common.
Whichever one you use:

- *Choose Early.* Most webinar platforms offer tutorials to get you started, but give yourself at least a month to practice with the technology before launching webinars of your own.

- *Avoid products that require users to install software.* Workplaces often have company firewalls that won't allow users to download applications without an administrator password. Unless you are getting technical assistance with your webinar, choose a platform with web-based interfaces that avoid this problem.

- *Get a platform that allows voice to be sent online (Known as VoIP—Voice over Internet Protocol).* VoIP allows your participants to listen in without tying up a phone line. It also makes it easier to record the webinar with audio.

Step 2: Create your presentation.

Most webinars are expanded from PowerPoint or Prezi slideshows, because speakers are comfortable with those tools. Slideshows offer a good starting point, but if you're starting from scratch, remember to incorporate the same design principles in slides for a webinar as for a traditional presentation.

- *Keep text to a minimum and use a large font size.* It's as boring to read a slide during a webinar as it is in a traditional presentation.

- *Use lots of big, bright visuals, to* illustrate your point. If participants will not see video of you during the webinar, show a picture of yourself. Pictures of the presenters are an excellent idea, as they help build a bond with the audience.

- *Use lots of slides.* Because slides are your main way of conveying motion, use a few more than a traditional presentation, to keep your audience involved. Olivia Mitchell, creator of www.speakingaboutpresetning.com suggests using twice as many slides as for a face-to-face presentation to keep things moving.[10]

- *Don't try anything too complex*, especially the first time around. Webinars are better suited to clear, concise presentations.

Step 3. Plan your timing.

Webinars should be short and focused. Most participants prefer an hour or less. That generally means about 40 minutes of content, 5 minutes of set up, and 15 minutes for questions.

Be sure to include:

- *An explanation of how the webinar will work.* Keep this short as people don't like long introductions.

- *Time for questions*, in the middle of the presentation and at the end as well.

- *A few questions that you can set up as polls* (where the audience clicks their vote). This technique gives you structured feedback and gets people involved in the talk.

Step 4: Invite people.

Send out announcements approximately a month before the event, and then a reminder at two weeks and one week.

To expedite registrations:

- *Keep your e-mail invitation short*, with a brief summary of the topic and a large, bold link to your registration page (which your webinar platform will help you set up).

- *Ask for as little information as possible, when people register.* Their name, e-mail address, and (possibly) their organization is all you should normally need. More questions will scare people away.

Step 5: Determine your space.

You need to have the right physical and virtual space to run a successful webinar. Here's what you need:

- *A room with a door.* A quiet space is important when you are presenting.

- *A good headset and microphone.* You can use the built in microphone on your computer, but this may produce an annoying feedback loop when the sound comes through your speakers and back into the computer's microphone. A headset with a microphone allows you to speak normally without the "echo."

Figure 5.12 Headset with Microphone

- *A hard wired Internet connection.* Wireless networks can sometimes drop connections or cause fuzzy audio. This is even more important, if you will also be using a webcam or some video transmission. Depending on the size of your audience, you may also want to encourage the participants to "attend" using a hard wired connection as well. Our experience with wireless access to a meeting link, or a Skype conference, has been less than stellar. Pay particular attention to this detail, if you are being interviewed via a video conference.

- *A clean virtual desktop.* When you turn on the webinar software's desktop, the users will be able to see everything that's on your screen. Make sure to close all windows except for your presentation files.

Step 6: Find a partner to moderate.

The moderator is important to review questions and deal with technical issues, which frees you to focus on your voice and your slides. Ideally, the moderator should be in a different room, using a different Internet connection. This ensures that if one connection has problems, someone will still be there to interact with the participants.

Step 7: Practice.

As with an in person presentation, it is very important to test the hardware and software well before the presentation. Ask a few friends to participate, ideally using different kinds of computers and Internet browsers.
  Look for:

- *Audio problems.* Some breakup is inevitable when sending audio online, but things like beeping noises on login or overly quiet vocals can be solved, either by calling the teleconference provider or moving the microphone closer. When in doubt, err on the loud side. People can always turn the volume down, but can't always turn it up.

- *Interface problems.* Make sure the participants can always see the space for typing questions (if available on your platform).

- *Delay problems*, when you click from slide to slide.

Here are a few last general suggestions for planning a remote presentation:

■ Be sure to conduct your test run with the actual slides you intend to use during the webinar. Slides sometimes lose their formatting in certain platforms, which can result in badly scaled graphs and tables with no content.

■ If you will be sharing your screen (and slides), and you should share your screen, depending on the technical capabilities of your webinar platform and the participants' hardware, listeners may not see exactly what you see. The screen sharing function may have a difficult time keeping up with constant visual changes such as motion. Although previously we suggested using animation to help your audience see and understand your topic, if you are using the same PowerPoint slides for the webinar, you may need to reduce the animation effects. So before you use these same slides in the webinar, go through and change smooth-motion effects such as slow fades, fly-ins, and wipes into simple appear/disappear animations. Although they may not have quite the same impact, you have a much better chance of seeing the same thing your audience sees. An occasional fade or wipe effect may be okay if it's only in a small region of a slide. The same applies to transitions. Delete anything that isn't simple.

Whether you are "attending" a webinar, giving a sales demo using virtual meeting software, or presenting to a large audience with state of the art *Telepresence*™ technology, following the steps just presented, will help ensure you aren't "surprised" by technical issues. If you take these extra precautions, you will certainly feel more confident and your audience will appreciate the effort and respect you for it.

Table 5.2 provides a summary of our recommendations for what to do before you present.

TABLE 5.2 What To Do Before You Present

The Task	The Details
1. Call your contact	Clarify the details of the room and the technology.
2. Plan your attire	Consider your dress in relation to audio and video projection limitations.
3. Pack your accessories	Make sure you have all the items you'll need. Use our checklist to help you remember.
4. Practice with the technology	Try to rehearse your presentaiton, from beginning to end, using the actual equipment.
5. Plan for Remote/Virtual Presentations	Keep in mind the issues related to using a virtual/webinar platform: Creating your slides Timing your Presentation Inviting Participants Dealing with Space Limiations Using a Moderator

DURING THE PRESENTATION

You've confirmed the details with your contact, chosen your attire, packed everything you'll need, and practiced with the technology. Now you're ready to actually give the presentation you've worked so hard on.

Getting Started

No matter how long you've been presenting or how many speeches you've given, getting off to a strong start with technology will help you feel more comfortable and set the tone for a great presentation.

To ensure a smooth beginning:

- *Arrive early.* This one is pretty obvious but don't overlook it, because it's so obvious. Arriving early allows you plenty of time to locate your technical contact, deal with any last minute changes, make any necessary copies, or deal with any other problems that could arise when you add technology to a speech. You may have already practiced with the technology (as we advised earlier), but if that wasn't possible, now is your chance to rehearse before you present.

- *Open your software* and load your content.

- *Turn on* the projection monitor and/or control panel.

- *Check the volume again*, especially if your practice session was more than 24 hours earlier.

As soon as you're confident everything is working properly, return to your opening slide and make sure it's displayed as the audience arrives. You don't want to be running through your slides too close to the time your presentation should begin.

For a remote/virtual presentation, here are a few more steps to remember as you get started.

- *Turn off Email.* Close it entirely. If you just minimize email, then pop-up notifications could be displayed as new messages come in. Even if you don't have this notification activated, email still takes bandwidth away from your webinar when email comes in.

- *Clean up your space (real and virtual).* If you're presenting with a webcam, remember the participants will see you as well as what is directly behind you, so make sure that area is neat and uncluttered. Your virtual space should be orderly as well, including your desktop background. Switching between applications provides the opportunity for participants to view your computer background, so put any icons you won't need into a temporary folder and change your background to something simple during your presentation.

During the remote/virtual presentation, be sure to:

- *Speak loudly and vary your tone.* Your audience can't see you, so your voice has to hold their attention.

- *Speak slowly.* Especially over VoIP, vocals get a bit garbled. Slowing down your speech will help with that problem.

Now you have begun the presentation and the speech is moving along well. The next challenge is to create opportunities for the listeners to become more involved in your presentation.

Promoting Audience Involvement

The advent of technology has changed the way we give presentations and, even more important, what audiences expect from a presentation. No longer can speakers expect to create a few slides and talk for 45 minutes, while the audience sits quietly taking notes. Certainly, some dynamic speakers capture the audience's attention simply because what they have to say is riveting and their delivery is dynamic. Steve Jobs hardly used any visual aids other than a few images displayed on a large screen behind him, and yet he was known as a very powerful speaker. But, he was Steve Jobs, so people listened. The rest of us won't have quite the same allure, so we will need to use any tools available to engage the audience and communicate our message. Even if you're not the keynote speaker at a TED conference (Technology, Entertainment, Design), you can still learn new ways to use technology to involve your audience in the presentation.

Promoting involvement and engagement is even more crucial when you are speaking to people you can't see, as with virtual meeting software such as *GoToMeeting©*, or *Adobe Connect©* or *Microsoft Live Meeting*. We can no longer simply rely on the traditional "one to many" mode of lecturing or speaking. With each passing year, more and more speakers are realizing they must adapt and change their speaking style to meet new audience expectations and fully utilize the available software tools. Technology provides new and exciting options to expand the "one-way" format of communication into a network of conversations that can occur:

Figure 5.13 Speaker to Audience

- Between the audience and the speaker (Figure 5.13)
- Between audience members (Figure 5.14)
- With people outside of the actual presentation (Figure 5.15)

Figure 5.14 Participant to Participant (Internal)

Figure 5.15 Participant to Participant (External)

Managing Remote/Virtual Presentations

Strategies to involve audiences are slightly different depending on the delivery platform you're using. Certainly strategies to engage people in a webinar or virtual meeting will work for an in person presentation, but remote presentations offer their own unique challenges. Since you often cannot see the audience (although they may see you), you cannot rely on non-verbal cues for feedback as to whether your message is being received. This lack of feedback means you need to frequently assess whether your listeners are still there and whether they're following along with the material.

To increase interaction between you and the remote participants, you can incorporate any of these suggestions in your presentation:

- *Ask an open ended question at the beginning of your presentation.* This is a good introductory strategy to help participants get involved with the technology and begin practicing with the chat window. An example would be, "How are you currently using social media in your courses?"

- *Answer questions as they come up.* This strategy keeps the audience engaged. Be sure to check the chat window frequently (where participants can type comments or questions for everyone else to see and respond to). Look for questions you can address as well, or let the moderator answer if you have one. If you can't get to a question, set it aside to answer after the webinar is over.

- *Ask specific questions to focus audience attention.* For example, instead of telling them why process A is better than B, ask, "What's the advantage of using A instead of B?" Then in your response to their comments, highlight the points you want to make.

- *Create a question slide.* Olivia Mitchell suggests speakers display a question on a slide and then discuss its answer. This strategy is particularly useful when the new question represents a change of topic from the previous slide.[11]

- *Ask "polling" questions.* This strategy gets the audience involved, but it also gives you structured feedback about their real time experience of your presentation.

- *Use animation to draw your listener's attention to your point.* The participants cannot see where you're pointing, so you need to create an animation to simulate what you would do in a face-to-face presentation.

Managing In-Person Presentations

Many options are available for speakers to interact *with*, as opposed to simply talk *to*, an in-person audience. As always, depending on your purpose, occasion, and audience, you can decide what will work best for you. Two electronic options are audience response systems and back channels.

Using Audience Response Systems

Audience Response Systems (ARS) currently are a popular way to involve the audience. ARS systems are a simple way to gather data about your listeners while you're speaking. An *ARS* is a computerized system by which the participants enter responses to questions using handheld devices. These devices transmit the individual responses back to a computer that instantly tabulates the data, and then

▼ **Audience Response System**
is a computerized system by which the participants enter responses to questions via handheld devices. The devices transmit the individual responses back to a computer that instantly tabulates the data, and then (typically) displays a summary of the results for the audience to review.

(typically) displays a summary of the results for the audience to review. ARS systems, such as electronic whiteboards (Figure 5.16), or "Clickers" (Figure 5.17), are widely used in presentations to:

- Solicit questions
- Obtain demographic information
- Conduct opinion polls
- Vote on ideas
- Quiz participants

Figure 5.16 Electronic Whiteboard

Figure 5.17 Clicker

How you choose to use an ARS in your presentation should be guided by what you'd like to know about your audience, but be creative. For the most part, an ARS is an efficient tool for conducting real time audience analysis to learn what the listeners already know about your topic, and what they would like to hear more about. Besides, most audiences really appreciate speakers reaching out to them directly and providing a means to get involved.

Automated Response Systems are easy to set up and use but do require additional expense and equipment, such as a terminal and the transmittal devices. Another software tool, with no hardware requirements other than what most speakers and listeners/participants already have, is a web-based service, found at www.polleverywhere.com. This service is free for audiences under 40 people and works internationally, using texting (SMS) on the web or Twitter. Figure 5.18 provides a screen shot of this free service.

The interactive *polleverywhere* application offers many of the same features as an ARS, and it can be used by the audience to ask questions of the speaker or a panel. This method is particularly effective for presentations when it may be difficult for the speaker to see everyone or when listeners may feel too intimidated to speak out. Any text or tweet from a listener is displayed on the screen for the audience to see. But as you can imagine, this is a double-edged sword. While seeing the comments on the screen provides excellent feedback for a speaker to modify a presentation, it also allows for negative or hostile comments to appear. *Polleverywhere* does offer a fee-based optional upgrade that allows the speaker to review texts or tweets before they appear on the screen. This option, called *Moderation*, can help prevent profanity, abusive, or embarrassing comments about you or your organization. Other web-based polling software is also available though, as of this writing, *polleverywhere* is one of the more popular.

From WWW.POLLEVERYWHERE.COM. Reprinted by permission.

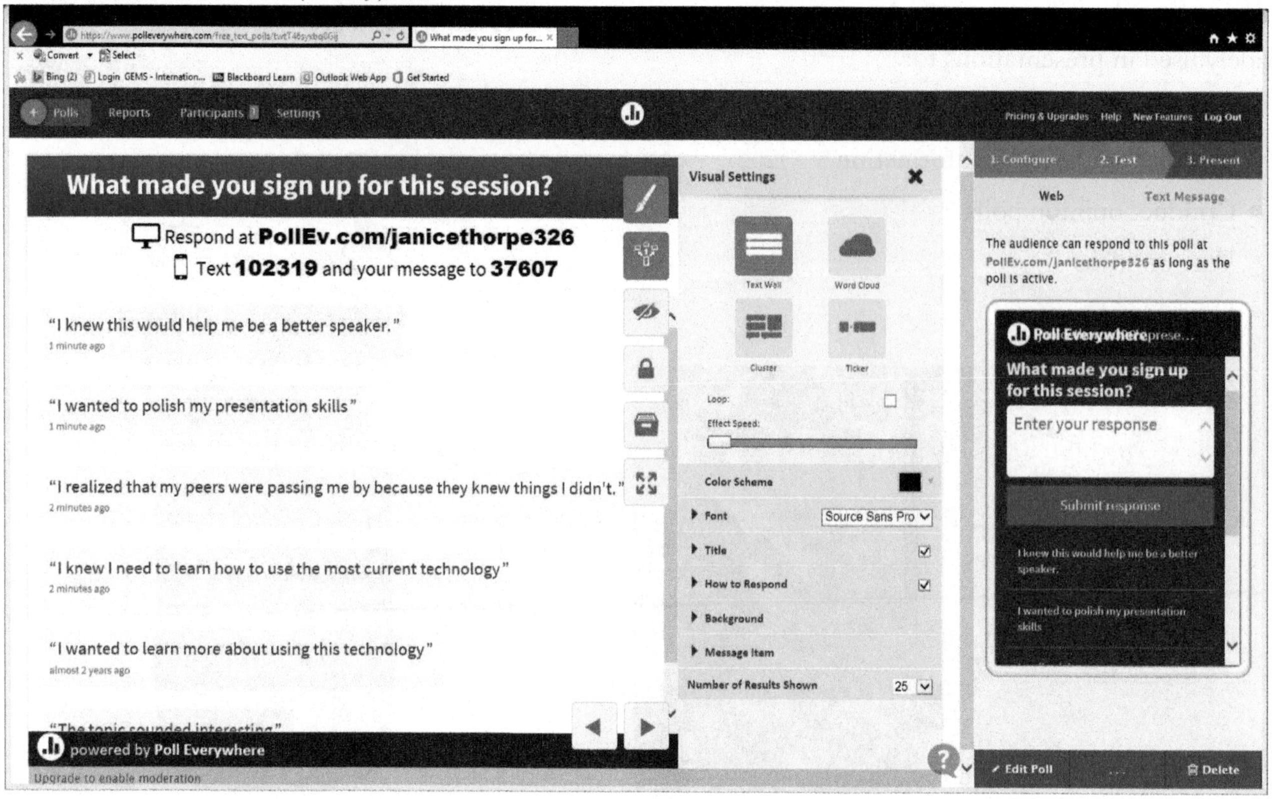

Figure 5.18 Screenshot of www.polleverywhere.com

Using a Backchannel

An ARS system focuses primarily on enhancing the feedback loop between the audience and the speaker, but it doesn't easily allow audience members to communicate with one another or with others not in the room. There are electronic tools that a public speaker can use to facilitate communication:

- Between audience members
- With people outside of the actual presentation

A speaker might choose to create space for a "*Backchannel*," which allows for communication outside what occurs traditionally between the speaker and the listeners. A **backchannel** is a "line of communication created by people in an audience to connect with others inside or outside the room, with or without the knowledge of the speaker."[12]

Any teacher or experienced presenter will tell you that *backchannels* have always existed. Students have whispered to one another in the classroom, audience members passed notes, and more recently, people text each other from various locations inside and outside the room. All of these are forms of the backchannel, but ever-expanding technology has taken this to a more exciting level and offers speakers a chance to participate in the *backchannel* as opposed to being unaware of what is being said, "behind your back."

Many tools are available to create a backchannel and more will be created, as people become more accustomed to participating in the expanded public speaking network. Some tools will be more useful for you than others, depending on your particular needs, but currently the most commonly used tool is Twitter.

▼ **A Backchannel** is a line of communication created by people in an audience to connect with others inside or outside the room, with or without the knowledge of the speaker.

> ## BOX 5.1
>
> ### WHAT YOU MIGHT BE THINKING ABOUT BACK CHANNELING DURING YOUR NEXT SPEECH!
>
> "If I open up all those channels, how will I control the content and flow of my presentation?"
>
> "I'm not sure I can keep track of all the streams of conversation."
>
> "What if someone starts an argument? How will I deal with a hostile listener?"
>
> "What if someone misinterprets something I've said, and tweets out to the world?"
>
> "What if the audience stops paying attention to what I'm saying?"
>
> "I'm a pretty dynamic speaker, so do I really need to do this?"
>
> "Backchanneling sounds really interesting, but it also scares me to death."

In one study of regular Twitter users attending the South by SouthWest conference (SXSW) in 2010, researchers found that Twitter usage increased significantly during the week of the conference,[13] which highlights Twitter's role as part of the backchannel trend.

After reading the last couple of paragraphs, and as a public speaker, you're probably thinking any, or most of, the hypothetical thoughts shown in Box 5.1.

These are all legitimate concerns and represent most of the risks of using a backchannel. Actually, most of these reactions are similar to risks any speaker might experience when giving a presentation, even before PowerPoint and Twitter. In any public speaking situation, for example, the speaker takes the risk of losing control of the audience or the listeners not paying attention. The strategies to deal with the potential risks of using a backchannel are similar to what any speaker would employ in a traditional presentation. We can condense these risks into three main areas and offer guidelines to help you feel more comfortable incorporating a backchannel.

1. What if I Lose Control of my Audience?

The first two thoughts in Box 5.1 focus on a change in the flow of a presentation. Traditionally, speakers talk and the audience follows along with the slides and possibly asks a few questions at the end of the presentation. With a backchannel, this process is upended, because you may have switched to the next point but audience members are still tweeting/blogging about your previous point. It's very similar to what happens when two people begin a separate, side conversation in the back of the room. Instead of everyone following along with you, those two listeners are talking about something different, but possibly related to your topic. In the past, people around them may have hushed the two talkers; but now, it may not be whispers you hear but the tapping of keys, as people tweet or post comments about your topic. Some of your listeners may even be having a conversation that the rest of the audience would benefit from hearing, and this will require you to determine how you can use this *side conversation* to enhance your presentation? The question now is, "How can I *direct* the flow of the presentation, not "How can I *control* it."

Here's how:

■ *Adjust your role to act more as a facilitator rather than a speaker.*

To help you maintain control of the presentation, but meet your audience's needs, you need to shift your role from speaker to facilitator. With the addition of a backchannel—which fosters interaction between you and the audience, and the audience members themselves—your job is not to stifle the network of communication, but to encourage it. Much like a facilitator for a meeting, or a group brainstorming session, adding a backchannel requires you to *manage* the interaction, not *control* it.

Managing a backchannel begins with acknowledging it exists. In this environment, it is okay to "pass notes," but with the intent of adding to the *conversation*. As the speaker, your job, kind of in this order, is to:

■ Invite the audience to participate

■ Listen for themes

■ Prompt others to comment

■ Summarize what you are hearing

When listeners feel their contributions are welcomed, and they can influence what is covered, they will be much more interested in what you have to say than if you pretend to already know what they want.

Adjusting your role also includes deciding *how* to manage all of the comments and content that might result from an audience's tweets or blogs. Cliff Atkinson, a professional speaker with years of experience using technology in presentations, suggests that, during any presentation, a speaker needs to take approximately three **"twitter breaks."**[14]

> ". . . you create the opportunity to involve your audience at the end of each section. You should involve them a minimum of three times within a typical 45 minute presentation."[15]

Incorporating these breaks allows you, the speaker, to gather feedback to adjust your content if necessary. You could also share the comments with the audience as a way of reengaging them after the break. Displaying these comments during the break requires you to either toggle between your presentation software and the backchannel tool (*Twitter/ Backnoise*, etc.), or use presentation software that shows the feed within the slides themselves (*Keynote Tweet*). You can use this information to decide whether to proceed with your content as you planned, or adjust your direction based on the feedback.

2. *How Should I Deal with Negative Comments?*

Concerns about possible conflict or dealing with potential negativity are also valid. One early example of audience negativity occurred in 2008 at the SXSW conference when the keynote interview of Mark Zuckerberg (CEO, Facebook) did not progress as the audience expected[16]. The listeners used the backchannel to voice their dissatisfaction and the tension came to a head when, during opening questions, a member of the audience asked a question of Mr. Zuckerberg, but the interviewer (Sarah Lacey) answered instead. The person asking the question interrupted Ms. Lacey and tersely said he wasn't asking her, but was talking to Mr. Zuckerberg.

The rest of the audience clapped and cheered. For several days after this debacle, the Internet was full of commentary about what happened, how the whole affair was handled, and what could be learned from it. To see the interview and commentary, go to http://www.wired.com/underwire/2008/03/sxsw-mark-zucke/.

Yes, there is the possibility that someone in the audience will be unhappy with something about your presentation. A listener might be offended by something you said, disagree with your perspective, or just be in a bad mood. Anytime you put your work or ideas out for comment, you run the risk of negative feedback. This is true in almost any occupation, in any field or industry. Some say, in fact, that "The best way to ruin a good idea is to take it to a meeting!" Indeed, if you offer your opinion in a meeting, a co-worker may make a snide remark. If you lead a training session, the evaluations may come back with criticism. If you teach a class, students may make unflattering comments about your teaching style or the content. Obviously, these reactions are not limited to presentations with a backchannel. Any presentation has the potential for audience dissatisfaction, with or without technology. Some of the reactions you can control and some you can't. But as with most risks, being prepared will go a long way to help you "keep your cool."

With a combined 40 years of teaching and speaking experience, we offer this advice:

- *Don't take it personally.*

  This is the most important piece of advice we can offer. Recognize that some listeners may have a different view, or different experiences with your topic or content, but learning how to receive feedback is an important skill for presenters. Certainly it can be a little painful to read that others were not wildly enthusiastic about your topic, but viewing this feedback as constructive rather than hurtful can actually help improve your presentation. Using the feedback, to objectively examine which comments have merit and which don't, will ultimately result in a stronger, more effective presentation. As university professors, we receive hundreds of course evaluations every year, and at first it's hard to process the negative comments. Eventually though we all learn to determine which comments are valid and require us to adjust our content or presentation methods.

- *Decide when you should address the negativity and when you should ignore it.*

  Whether you decide to address any negative comments from the backchannel (or in some cases directly from a participant) really is up to you and how comfortable you feel with the particular audience, and your topic. Although there is no single set of criteria for speakers to follow, Atkinson offers several guidelines to help determine how to handle negative or snarky comments[17].

Ignore negative comments when:

- The comment only applies to a small number of listeners
- They aren't related to the topic
- You don't feel you would handle the situation well
- Addressing the comment would just add unnecessary distraction

- You can't change anything

Address negative comments when:

- The comment applies to a large number of audience members
- The commenter is disrupting your presentation
- You feel the need to protect or defend your reputation
- You can do something about the comment, as in a misunderstanding

The 2008 SXSW interview of Mark Zuckerberg met the above criteria for a negative comment that should be addressed. Had the interviewer been aware of and acknowledged what was happening in the backchannel, the interview might have been handled far differently.

As a speaker in the 21ˢᵗ century, you have a choice to make. You can choose to ignore the backchannel, hope it won't be a disruption, and present the same way you always have. Your other choice is to acknowledge the backchannel and figure out how to best use it to enhance your presentation. If you choose option one, it's likely you will be frustrated and audiences will be bored. Remember, you audience is increasingly wired and expects more. Option two, acknowledging the backchannel, will help you connect with your audience, and ultimately improve your presentation. Having taught basic public speaking for more than 20 years, we have always instructed students to *have a conversation* with the audience, and a backchannel expands the concept of a conversation to include electronic communication as well.

3. But Do I Really Need to Go to All this Trouble?

Yes. That's the simple answer. But the bigger question is *"Why should I go through all this effort"*? The answer lies back at the beginning of this part of our book—because audience expectations have changed, and therefore, as speakers, we must change and adapt as well. We are not suggesting you have to completely change your presentation style or methods, but only that you begin to experiment with the tools and applications that will enhance your presentations and allow you to reach even more listeners, through ever expanding channels. As we said previously, audiences can get almost any kind of information, from many different sources, but presentations, meetings, and lectures offer opportunities for participants to interact with one another, and interaction is what they can't get anywhere else. Your job is to help make this happen. Ultimately, the goal of a speaker is to communicate some message or information to an audience. The platforms to deliver your message have expanded and evolved, so this means you need to expand and evolve as well.

Chris Brogan, a frequent presenter on maximizing the backchannel, deals with all forms of *Twitter* comments during his talks, whether positive or negative. "Speakers need to know that people want to be heard. They want to be accounted for in conversations. You have to be flexible," says Brogan. Even if you ignore individual posts during your presentation, Brogan suggests you address some of them with your audience before or after your presentation. You can watch a full video of Chris Brogan addressing negative comments that had been building up all day before he was scheduled to present at the New Media Atlanta conference in 2009. www.chrisbrogan.com/what-I-told-them-at-new-media-atlanta. (Recorded by Run Level Media—Atlanta)

And, for more suggestions on incorporating a backchannel into your presentation, see *The BackChannel: How Audiences are Using Twitter and Social Media and Changing Presentations Forever* (2010), by Cliff Atkinson. An excellent companion reference is Olivia Mitchell's ebook called *How to Present with Twitter* available from http://speakingaboutpresenting.com/wp-content/uploads/Twitter.pdf.

This discussion covered a lot of information about what to do during your presentations. Table 5.3 below provides a summary of our recommendations.

TABLE 5.3 What To Do During the Presentation

Cause	Reaction
6. Getting started	Arrive early, check your equipment and close any programs or files you won't need.
7. Promoting audience involvement Remote/virtual presentations In-person presentations	Ask open ended questions and answer questions as they arise. Use a question slide to keep participants on track. Consider using an Audience Response System (ARS), or Backchannel

AFTER THE PRESENTATION

Now that the presentation is over, it's time to consider how well it was received. The mark of any good presenter is asking for feedback in order to improve the presentation, both in content and delivery. There are several important steps you need to take after your presentation is over. Whether it was a face-to-face presentation or a webinar, you can still continue the connection with your audience, especially if it was a one-time event.

Step 1: Distribute Speaker Evaluation Forms

Evaluation forms are invaluable tools to help you determine if your content matched the audience's needs and met their expectations, and what areas could be improved. You can distribute evaluations at the end of the presentation session, but try to allow time for people to fill them out before they leave in order to maximize the quality of the feedback. Keep the form simple and limit it to a single page. If you used a backchannel, be sure to review it as well for information on improving your presentation.

In addition to paper forms, you may want to send a link to a web-based survey (such as *Survey Monkey or SurveyGizmo*) after the presentation. At these websites, you can create your own evaluation survey that contains the questions you want to ask. This approach gives people more time to think about their responses and may alleviate concerns about anonymity. The disadvantage is that it is likely to reduce your response rate as well. Offering both paper and electronic channels gives your listeners the option that works best for them.

When you get the evaluations back, separate the responses into things you can control, and things you can't and thoughtfully consider how you can use the information to improve your presentation. If you used a backchannel, be sure to review those comments as well. Comments from a backchannel are likely to be different but may offer information you've never had before. Don't be too concerned about the number of comments, because it could mean that you were so engaging that participants didn't have time to send any.

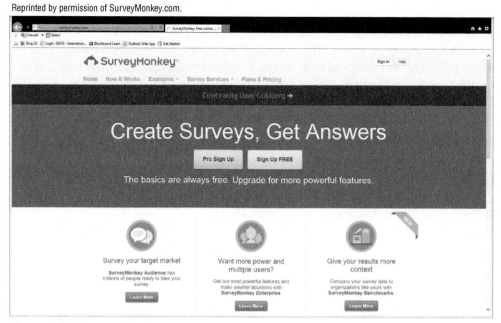

Figure 5.19 Survey Monkey

BOX 5.2

Speaker Evaluation Form

For the statements below, indicate whether you agree or disagree using the following scale:

SA = Strongly Agree   SA = Strongly Agree   D = Disagree   SD = Strongly Disagree

1. The speaker was organized. I could follow the content easily.

SA	A	Undecided	D	SD

2. The speaker promoted audience interaction by asking questions

SA	A	Undecided	D	SD

3. The speaker promoted audience interaction using technology (clickers, polling, etc.).

SA	A	Undecided	D	SD

4. The speaker began and ended on time.

SA	A	Undecided	D	SD

5. The speaker was interesting to listen to.

SA	A	Undecided	D	SD

(Continued)

BOX 5.2 Continued

6. The speaker had good delivery skills (gestures, voice, eye contact).

SA	A	Undecided	D	SD

7. The visual aids (if applicable were clear and easy to read)

SA	A	Undecided	D	SD

8. The speaker presented the information I expected to hear.

SA	A	Undecided	D	SD

The speaker was well-prepared with all relevant materials

SA	A	Undecided	D	SD

10. The session objectives were met.

SA	A	Undecided	D	SD

11. What was the best idea you heard in today's session.

Box 5.2 contains a possible speaker evaluation form that you could modify to suit your own needs. The questions are based on the speech evaluation form (the Competent Speaker) distributed by the National Communication Association.

Step 2: Answer any questions you didn't get to during the presentation.

This can take place in several different ways, depending on how your presentation was delivered. For example, in a face-to-face presentation, you can move to a different area or room for further questions. Another option, particularly if you used a remote platform, is to offer an online question and answer session once you finish your presentation. You can answer more questions and in greater depth in using this approach.

Step 3: Send a link to additional resources.

Participants will appreciate quick access to any information you mentioned during your presentation. If you gave a webinar and it was recorded, be sure to include this link as well. If you used a backchannel, you could also send a copy of the comments. The key is to follow through and maintain some kind of connection with your audience. If you maintain a blog or website, put the links and comments there as well. Of course, before the presentation is over, let the audience know about these follow up resources and how to access them.

Step 4: Send a thank you note.

Although this last step may seem unimportant, it's not. Sending a thank you note to the conference organizer, or the person who invited you to speak, is a considerate and professional touch that will be remembered long after your speech. A handwritten note is best, but email is better than no note at all.

TABLE 5.4 What To Do After the Presentation

Cause	Reaction
8. Evaluating the presentation	Pass out an evaluation form or consider online evaluations
9. Engaging in follow up	Send a link for further resources, and a thank you note to the conference organizer.

Table 5.4 provides a summary of our recommendations for what to do when your presentation is over.

In this final part of our book, we offered some new perspectives on today's audiences, and we described some changes in listeners' expectations of public speakers. We invite you now to consider what this means for you as a speaker. We also provided guidelines for using some exciting new tools for connecting with today's audiences. But, we didn't provide exercises for this final discussion, because they aren't really relevant. All of the information and suggestions we just provided can only be implemented as your prepare for your next presentation or webinar. Rather than give you exercises, our best advice, to paraphrase a tag line from Nike, is—*Just Go Do It!*

We certainly hope we've stimulated your thinking about technology and how you can integrate it into your presentations. By the time you are reading this, the last page of this book, yet more new presentation technologies will probably be available. Their use is both exciting and maybe a bit intimidating. We are fully confident you will embrace their use as a well-informed, highly competent 21st century public speaker.

GLOSSARY

Audience Response System is a computerized system by which the participants enter responses to questions via handheld devices. The devices transmit the individual responses back to a computer that instantly tabulates the data, and then (typically) displays a summary of the results for the audience to review.

Backchannel is a line of communication created by people in an audience to connect with others inside or outside the room, with or without the knowledge of the speaker.

Digital natives are teens and twenty-somethings, (born after 1990) who have never known a world without laptops, cell phones and 24/7 connectivity.

Hashtag is a word or phrase prefixed with the symbol "#" that is a form of a metadata tag. A hashtag is commonly used to group information and link it to a searchable phrase that returns any context that includes the hashtag, for example, 21st century Presentations.

Webinar is a combination of the words **web**cast and seminar. A presentation, delivered online, using visuals, the presenter's voice, and interactive elements to bring people together for training, information, and collaboration.

ENDNOTES

[1] Dobson, L. (2010). The net generation. *Therapy Today*, 21 (4), pp. 28–31.

[2] Loy, D. (2010). *The Y Generation: They're Coming; Are We Ready?*,
Facilities Manager, pp. 42–46.

[3] Bell, C. (2007). *The Impact of Meetings on Adult Education and How Technology is Changing It.* Retrieved from Corbin Ball Associates—The Meeting Technology Professionals: http://www.corbinball.com/articles_technology/index.cfm?fuseaction=cor_av&artID=5537

[4] Atkinson, C. (2010). *The Backchannel: How Audiences are Using Twitter and Social Media and Changing Presentations Forever.* Berkeley, CA: New Riders.

[5] Frost, D. (2008). *Welcome to Conference 2.0*, CNN Money, March 11, 2008. Retrieved from http://money.cnn.com/2008/03/11/technology/fost_conference.fortune/?postersin=2008031115

[6] *How to Host a Successful Webinar.* (n.d.). Retrieved from Effective Meetings.com: http://www.effectivemeetings.com/technology/conferencing/success_webinars.asp

[7] World Trade Group Limited. (2011, January). *wtg News.* Retrieved from http://www.wtgnews.com/2011/01/who-what-where-why-webinar-2/

[8] World Trade Group Limited. (2011, January). *wtg News.* Retrieved from http://www.wtgnews.com/2011/01/who-what-where-why-webinar-2/

[9] *www. communitysector.nl.ca.* (2011). Retrieved from Community Sector Council Newfoundland and Labrador.

[10] Mitchell, O. (2010, September 30). *18 Tips on How to Conduct an Engaging Webinar.* Retrieved from Speaking about Presenting: http://www.speakingaboutpresenting.com/presentation-skills/how-to-conduct-engaging-webinar/

[11] Mitchell, O. (2010, September 30). 18 Tips on How to Conduct an Engaging Webinar. Retrieved from Speaking about Presenting: http://www.speakingaboutpresenting.com/presentation-skills/how-to-conduct-engaging-webinar/

[12] Atkinson, C. (2010). *The Backchannel: How Audiences are Using Twitter and Social Media and Changing Presentations Forever.* Berkeley, CA: New Riders.

[13] Vega, E., Parthasaranthy, R., Torres, J. (June 1, 2010). *Social Couch: Musings on Social Media and Web.* Retrieved from http://www.socialcouch.com/twitter usage-at-conferences/

[14] Atkinson, C. (2010). *The Backchannel: How Audiences are Using Twitter and Social Media and Changing Presentations Forever.* Berkeley, CA: New Riders.

[15] Atkinson, C. (2010). *The Backchannel: How Audiences are Using Twitter and Social Media and Changing Presentations Forever.* Berkeley, CA: New Riders.

[16] Wallace, L. March 9, 2008. *Underwire: The Beat Goes On.* Wired Magazine. Retrieved from http://www.wired.com/underwire/2008/03/sxsw-mark-zucke/

[17] Atkinson, C. (2010). *The Backchannel: How Audiences are Using Twitter and Social Media and Changing Presentations Forever.* Berkeley, CA: New Riders.

Index

Note: "Figures are indicated by an italic *f*; tables are indicated by an italic *t*; notes are indicated by an italic *n*."

A

Alignment, 41–42, 45*t*
Align objects, 70*f*
Animation
  add emphasis effect, 87–89
  adjust object effects, 86–87
  chart, graph/*SmartArt* object, 89–90
  create bullet points, 85–86
  reorder bullet points, 86
Animation Pane, 86–88
Animation Timing, 88*f*
Arnston, A., 40*n7*
Arrow Width options, 105
ARS. *See* Audience response systems (ARS)
Atkinson, C., 126*n4*, 140*n12*, 142*n14*,
  142*n15*, 143*n17*
Attribution licenses, 28*t*
Audience response systems (ARS), 138–139
Audio playback options, 78*f*
Avatar, 116

B

Backchannel
  definition, 140
  feedback improve presentation, 143
  goal of speaker, 144
  ignore negative comments, 143–144
  negative comments, 142–143
  side conversation, 141–142
  Twitter, 140
Background options, 72–73
Background sound, Prezi, 108–109
BackNoise, 126, 142
Bar charts, 51–52, 80, 81
Behnke, R.R., 10*n4*
Bell, C., 125*n3*
Brumberger, E., 21*n3*
Building presentations. *See* PowerPoint
  (PPT); Prezi

C

Canvas, 101, 102
Chart Animation, 89*f*
"Chart junk," 29, 80, 82
Child, J.T., 9*n3*
Clicker, 113, 131, 139*f*
Cloud-based applications, 98
CMYK model, 40
Column charts, 80, 89
Competent public speaking
  anxiety (*see* Public speaking anxiety)
  definition, 1
  ethical communication, 3
  ethical responsibilities, 12, 14*t*
  NCA's model (*see* NCA's competent
    speaker model)
  "pet peeves," 12–13, 13*t*
Contrast, 37–40, 45*t*
"Creative Commons," 28
Custom slide show, 90–92
Cyphert, D., 21*n5*

D

Data Labels, 80, 82, 97
Data visualization, 49–50, 55–56
Delivering presentations
  additional resources, 147
  answer audiences questions, 147
  audiences expectations, 124
  audiences response, 125–126
  call to contact, 129–130
  competencies, 124*t*
  distribute speaker evaluation forms, 145–147
  free online learning opportunities, 125
  get start, 136
  managing in-person presentations, 138–140
  managing remote/virtual presentations, 138
  pack accessories, 131
  plan attire, 130–131

Delivering presentations (*Continued*)
  practice with technology, 131–132
  promoting audience involvement, 137
  recommendations, 148
  remote/virtual presentations, planning,
    132–135
  thank you note, 147
  using backchannel (*see* Backchannel)
  webinar, 127–129
Designing presentations. *See Simplicity, Contrast,*
    Repetition, Alignment, and *Proximity* ("*SCRAP*")
    approach
Diagram, 53
Dickson, G.W., 22*n8*, 23*n10*
Dickson O.W., 35*n2*
Digital natives, 125
Digital visual literacy
  create visually appealing presentation aids, 20
  software tools, 21*f*
  visual aids, 20, 22–23
Dobson, L., 125*n1*
Dreamstime, 28
Duarte, N., 35*n1*
Dykes, B., 36*n5*, 48*n5*

E

Electronic Whiteboard, 139*f*
Endersby J., 48*n8*
Ethical communication, 3

F

Facebook, 26, 27, 124
Face-to-face presentations (f2f), 126,
    133, 145, 147
Fade-in Animation, 112*f*
Festinger, L., 24*n13*
Flammia, M., 27*n16*
Flemming, N., 22*n9*
Flowchart, 52–53
Fonts, 47–48
Format Data Point, 83
Frames, Prezi, 102–103
Frost, D., 126*n5*
Frymier, A.B., 9*n4*

G

Group objects, 71*f*
Gurak, L.J., 50*n12*, 53*n13*

H

Hashtag, 130
Hyperlink, 73–74
Hyperlink colors, 75*f*

I

Iconic representation, 26–27
Invite to Edit, 115
ISO symbols, 27*f*
iStockphoto, 28

K

Kahl, D.H. Jr., 9*n3*
Keywording, 46
Kravik, R.B., 21*n4*

L

Lapel microphone, 130*f*
Lehman, J.A., 22*n8*, 23*n10*, 35*n2*
Line graph, 51, 80–81
Login Screen, Prezi, 98
Loy, D., 125*n2*

M

Machlis, S., 56*n15*
Marcus, A., 48*n9*
Media Toolbar, 76*f*
  add Bookmark, 77–78
  edit Video, 76–77
  insert Audio, 78
  insert Table, 79–80
  insert Video, 76
  Trim Video, 77
Microsoft®, 20
Mills, C., 22*n9*
Mitchell, O., 133*n10*, 138*n11*
Moore, M., 3*n2*
Morreale, S.P., 1*n1*, 3*n2*
Munter, M., 49*n10*

N

National Communication Association (NCA), 3
NCA's competent speaker model, 3
  chooses and narrows topic, 4–5
  communicating nonverbally, 8–9

communicating, own voice, 8
determine thesis/specific purpose, 5
organizing and outlining, 6–7
researching and supporting, 5–6
use appropriate language, 7–8

O

Oppenheim, L., 22*n*7, 23*n11*
Organization chart, 53
Oulton, N., 25*n14*, 26*n15*

P

Paradi, D., 49*n10*
Parallelism, 46–47
Parthasaranthy, R., 141*n13*
Path, 109–111
Pearson, J.C., 9*n3*
Picture superiority effect, 24, 25
Pie charts, 52, 81–84
Polleverywhere, 139–140
PowerPoint (PPT), 20, 63–64
    add animation (*see* Animation)
    add media (*see* Media Toolbar)
    add narration, 93–94
    add transitions, 90–91
    align text boxes/objects, 70
    change background, 72–73
    create bar chart/line graph, 80–81
    create custom slide show, 90–92
    create pie charts, 81–84
    create return link, 75
    crop picture, 68*f*
    display custom show, 92
    edit bar chart/line graph, 81
    edit text box, 66–67
    group multiple objects, 71
    insert Hyperlink, 73–74
    insert Screenshot, 68–69
    insert Toolbar, 67*f*
    Print Screen function, 69–70
    record slide timing, 92
    save formatted picture/image, 70
    self-running presentations, 92–93
    Slide Master, 65–66
    templates, 66
    use Smart Art, 71–72
Prezi, 63–64
    accessing Prezi files, 99
    add arrow, 105

add audio, 108–109
add Fade-in Animation, 112*f*
autoplay, 114
canvas, 101
cloud-based applications, 98
create new Prezi, 100
create path, 110–111
crop image, 104–105
download options, 113–114
File Options bar, 113, 116*f*
frames, 102–103
group objects, 103
insert images, 104
inserting pictures and objects, 103–104
insert Layout, 110
insert PowerPoint slides, 109
insert symbols and shapes, 105
Invite to Edit, 115
open account, 98
presentation options, 112
present button, 112
present remotely, 116
print Prezi, 114
privacy settings, 117–118
remote clicker, 113
templates, 99*f*
Text Editor, 101
themes menu, 106*f*
3D background, 107
transformation tool, 102
workspace, 100
Print Prezi, 114
Proximity, 43–44, 45*t*
Public Speaking 1.0, 1
Public Speaking 2.0, 1
Public speaking anxiety, 12*t*
    cause of, 10–12
    Roman orator, 9–10, 9*f*
    unlearning anxiety, 11

R

Repetition, 40–41, 45*t*
Return Link, 75*f*
Reynolds, G., 36*n4*, 37*n6*
RGB color model, 40

S

Sawyer, C.R., 10*n4*
Screenshot Cascade Window, 68, 69*f*

Self-running presentations, 92–93
Shutterstock, 28
Simplicity, 36–37, 45*t*
Simplicity, Contrast, Repetition, Alignment, and
    Proximity ("*SCRAP*") approach, 45*t*
  alignment, 41–42
  bar charts, 51–52
  contrast, 37–40
  data visualization, 49–50, 55–56
  diagram, 53
  flowchart, 52–53
  fonts, 47–48
  keywording, 46
  line graphs, 51
  maps and geographic data, 53–54
  organization chart, 53
  parallelism, 46–47
  pie chart, 52
  proximity, 43–44
  repetition, 40–41
  simplicity, 36–37
  structuring text, 45–46
  surface charts, 51
  tables, 50–51
  type size, 48–49
  visual aid redesign, 57–59
  Wi-Fi, 54–55
Singer, N., 55*n14*
Skype, 123, 124, 126, 132, 134
Slide Master, 65–66
Smart Art, 71–72
Smith, T.E., 9*n4*
Spalter, A., 19*n1*, 21*n6*
Surface charts, 51
Surges-Tatum, D., 3*n2*
Survey Monkey, 146*f*

T

Templates, 66, 99*f*
Themes menu, Prezi, 106*f*
3D background, 107

Torres, J., 141*n13*
Transformation Tool, 102
Transitions, 90–91
Trendalyzer, 55
Trigger, 88
Trim Video, 77
Tufte, E., 29*n17*, 49*n11*
Twitter, 55, 56, 126, 130, 139–142, 145
Type size, 48–49

V

van Dam, A., 19*n1*, 21*n6*
Vega, E., 141*n13*
Video formatting options, 77*f*
Video playback options, 76*f*
Vision science, 23–24
Visual aids, 20, 22–23
Visual cognitive dissonance, 24–25
Visualization
  design principles, 30–32
  digital visual literacy (*see* Digital
    visual literacy)
  find good images, 27–29
  iconic representation, 26–27
  Millennials and *Generation C,*
    19, 19f
  picture superiority effect, 24
  vision science, 23–24
  visual cognitive dissonance,
    24–25
Vogel, D.R., 22*n8*, 23*n10*, 35*n2*
Voss, D., 27*n16*

W

Wallace, L., 142*n16*
Webinar, 127–129
Webster, L., 3*n2*
Web 2.0 technologies, 125
Williams, R., 36*n3*
Workspace, Prezi, 100*f*